GREEN LEAVES

GREEN LEAVES

by

Mrs Robert Henrey

J. M. DENT & SONS LTD

LONDON

FROM THE AUTHORESS TO THE READER

The impact of a prospective daughter-in-law on her future husband's family is sometimes disconcerting. This is an account of conflicts that I, as a bride, once innocently set in motion. Some aspects of my husband's family are already known to my readers. If they are briefly recalled here, it is merely for the sake of clarity.

MADELEINE HENREY

Birth	THE LITTLE MADELEINE	Aug 13 1906
My father (Milou) *b.* 1873, dies	ditto	Apr 9 1921
Arrive alone aged 15 in London	ditto	Nov 1921
Mother (Matilda) follows		1922
Convent at Tooting	AN EXILE IN SOHO	1922
I work in a Soho newspaper shop	JULIA AND OTHERS	1922–3
Shopgirl at Galeries Lafayette	JULIA	1923–4
Typist to a silk merchant in City		1924
ditto at Gaumont, Denman St, Piccadilly		1925
I go with my mother to Paris to learn hairdressing	THE LITTLE MADELEINE	1925
I work in Coventry Street	A GIRL AT TWENTY	1926
Manicurist at the Savoy Hotel	MADELEINE GROWN UP	Feb–Dec 1927
First taken to Brentford to meet my future parents-in-law	GREEN LEAVES	1927
I fall ill and am sent by Robert to Pau		1928
Return in November—wedding at St George's, Hanover Square	MADELEINE GROWN UP	Dec 1 1928
We take an apartment in Beauchamp Place, Knightsbridge		1929
Effie and Burr leave Brentford and go to Godalming	GREEN LEAVES	1930
Girl diarist on London evening paper	ditto	1930–8
I buy the farm in Normandy		1937
Bobby born on the farm	MADELEINE YOUNG WIFE *Part One*	June 26 1939
Flee from the farm before advancing German army and return to London leaving Matilda on the quay	LONDON UNDER FIRE *and* MADELEINE YOUNG WIFE	1940
Burr dies at Godalming during the great raid on the City	GREEN LEAVES	Dec 31 1940
I return to Paris alone to find Paris just liberated—and my farm a scene of murder and desolation	LONDON UNDER FIRE *and* MADELEINE YOUNG WIFE *Part Two*	1945
Effie (*b.* May 15 1865) dies	GREEN LEAVES	1946
My mother (*b.* 1886) dies	HER APRIL DAYS	May 1962

I

HAVE YOU EVER CONSIDERED the emotions that can sometimes assail a young girl on her first visit to her prospective in-laws?

I did not try to picture the scene until the dawn of that Saturday morning when he came to fetch me in the one-room apartment which my mother and I shared in Stacey Street, Soho, looking as uncertain of himself as we were. He said that I must not judge what I was about to see by its immediate environment —a bottle-neck of trams, brewery drays, trucks and motor vans at Brentford, Middlesex, on the road to Hounslow and the West. I would have a shock, of course. There was a gasworks on one side which positively stank and a brewery on the other, and a little farther along, where Julius Caesar was said to have crossed the Thames at low tide (a stone column had been erected with a suitable inscription) was a soap factory that produced on occasion such nauseating smells that one had to pinch one's nose in passing. The Brentford High Street had been famous in history as the road to Bath. One might possibly, he said, balance its historical fame against its dirt and noise. His father, the Vicar of St George's church in the High Street (opposite the gasworks), had often seen King Edward VII held up in a royal motor car by a recalcitrant tram (the electric arm sometimes jumped clear of the overhead lines) between the church and the precise spot where the coal-heavers sat on a long bench with sacks over their heads and coal-dust all over their faces. As the gas workers were my future father-in-law's parishioners (and their wives members of my future mother-in-law's Bible Class), they smiled at the people from the vicarage whenever they passed by, even doffing their traditional headgear. And of course they enjoyed it immensely when King Edward and his beautiful Queen got stuck in the

7

royal car in the middle of the traffic. This was long before my time. King George V and Queen Mary were now on the throne.

Sometimes my fiancé slept at home, sometimes in town. On this occasion he came up especially to fetch me. The vicarage, he said, was seven miles from Hyde Park Corner. As a boy he had often walked it in the early morning, having nothing better to do, thanks to holidays from Oxford, for the fun of enjoying the colourful scene of Covent Garden market at 6 a.m., when the women in their bonnets and beaded black shawls were busy shelling peas. All along the road from Brentford, past Gunners-bury, Turnham Green and Hammersmith, he had been passed by carts bringing vegetables and fruit from the market gardens at Isleworth and Hounslow, the drivers asleep, leaving the shire horses to amble slowly along. At this hour of the morning the trams had barely begun to leave their depots, and traffic was at a minimum. This was something else I must bear in mind to offset the deplorable first impressions of the bottle-neck, the rich market gardens that were not immediately visible to the eye. His father, he said, owned a strawberry field, the income of which went towards the upkeep of the church, which was eternally poor.

Which of us was most nervous? The question is absurd. The girl, of course. He had chosen Saturday because he was then working on the *Morning Post* which had no Sunday paper. On Sunday he went to the office, then in the Strand, to work on Monday's edition. So Sunday would have been impossible. Sunday would have been equally difficult for my future in-laws, who from early Holy Communion to Evensong scarcely had a moment to themselves. Curiously enough they felt that though it was right for them to work on Sundays, it was wrong for their son to do so. Helping to produce a London morning paper was a secular occupation but so, of course, logically, was manning the gasworks or the waterworks, where Mr Stamp, the turncock, was one of the vicar's churchwardens.

If my fiancé and I, in our different ways, were nervous, so was my mother. With her usual pessimism, she said firmly: 'You'll see. It just won't work.' But as she was proud of her daughter, she added: 'Not that you're not worth ten of any man!' But a moment

8

later, she caught herself saying: 'I fear it will prove to be a wasted day, and bring unhappiness to all of us!'

I wanted to be extremely elegant—but not too elegant. I must not give the impression of being a coquette, or a girl who spends too much money on her clothes. The very idea made me smile. My mother made all my clothes. But on the other hand I must do credit to my clever mother, and I would not for all the world wish to appear dowdy. I would have to strike a sophisticated mean. The door-bell rang and emotion stifled me. What did all three of us really want?

'How do we go?' I asked, as he and I, after bidding farewell to my anxious mother, hurried down Stacey Street on our way to Charing Cross Road.

'By underground to Chiswick Park,' he said, 'and from there by tram. I hope you will be indulgent about lunch. It's sure to be dreadful. My mother never eats meat and has the impression that we all like it overdone, so it's generally a tough roast joint on Saturdays.'

'At least it will be hot,' I said, 'and anyway I shall be too nervous and shy to eat anything. Do you always have roast beef on Saturday?'

'It's on account of eating it cold on Sunday,' he said. 'The maids must be free to go to church if they want to. It's a ritual. Sunday lunch consists of cold meat and boiled potatoes, and pears or peaches out of a tin. We consume large quantities of California tinned fruit. My mother orders them with the groceries from what she calls "dear Harrods".'

'Must we take the underground?' I asked, as we turned into Trafalgar Square. 'The tube makes me feel sick. Are there no buses?'

'We could take a No. 9 from the Strand to Hammersmith and jump on a tram from there. That's where we join up with the river again. We are practically river folk.'

So we jumped on a No. 9 bus in front of Coutts Bank in the Strand and travelled half across London, past Knightsbridge barracks, Hyde Park, the Albert Hall, Kensington Gardens and Baron's Court to Hammersmith. Hammersmith Broadway was full of brightly lit shops and market stalls from which hung dresses, coats and stockings gently fluttering in the wind. Through all these clattered the largest, noisiest trams I have ever seen, great heavy things that made the London buses appear almost small. We boarded one bound for Hampton Court and climbed up to the top, from the front seat of which we had an admirable view of everything that lay before us. My fiancé explained that trams from Shepherd's Bush would join up with us before long and take the same route past Turnham Green, Chiswick and Brentford to Isleworth, where they again parted, some going as ours to Hampton Court, others to Hounslow, famous for Dick Turpin, the eighteenth-century highwayman who infested the road to Bath. His father had told him. . . .

Ah, I thought, perhaps his father will be the easiest to conquer. A father who liked to talk about Dick Turpin and kings of England who got stuck in traffic blocks in Brentford High Street. My future mother-in-law sounded more intimidating. In my naïveté I counted on my feminine charms to make an impression on the vicar. Here was Turnham Green church in the middle of the Green facing the famous Chiswick Empire, where George Robey and Little Tich played as in the London halls, Kew Bridge where one obtained the first glimpse of the wide eyot-dotted Thames and soon, past the waterworks into the bottle-neck half hidden under a mist of gas-ridden fumes. My fiancé was so nervous that he forgot to point out his father's church, but hurried me down the steep steps of the tram and onto the narrow pavement, where we paused for a moment in front of an ornamental iron gate painted green leading down into what appeared to be a shrubbery.

'The house is through there,' he said.

The dray-carts from the brewery with their sturdy shire horses plodded grimly between more modern forms of traffic. On the opposite side of the road was a baker's shop called Newens, behind the counter of which one could see a majestically bosomed woman whose ample rolled-up hair resembled in shape the cottage loaves that were exhibited in the window—loaves which consisted of two rounded blobs of golden baked bread, one balanced over the other like a Humpty Dumpty, all head and all tummy, sitting on a wall. 'Newens have been there ever since I was born,' he said. 'They also act as the Post Office. Are you dreadfully disappointed? I often feel very ashamed to let people know that I live in such a strange part of the world.'

'When I close my eyes,' I said, 'I smell the same smells that accompanied all my early girlhood. Only the language was different and instead of the Seine there is the Thames—or at least so I suspect because since Kew Bridge I have lost sight of it.'

'You will see,' he said, pushing open the iron gate that creaked on its unoiled hinges.

The slope as they called it, with evergreens and tall trees on either side, curved slightly, and then suddenly we were in a small forecourt facing the house, painted green, with pillars, Grecian style, framing a heavy front door. The house had hardly changed exteriorly since it was a farmhouse in the reign of Charles the First, and to the right of the forecourt was a low building that until quite recently had served as a laundry. All this was not at all what I expected. In truth at this moment, the knocker having been knocked, I stood there half in mockery, half in fear. A memory had been running through my head since I had seen from our wooden bench on top of the tram the church opposite the gasworks. One evening of the previous week I had gone as usual to buy three pairs of silk stockings from Etam in Piccadilly Circus, and I recognized the girl who served me as having worked with me when we were both salesgirls two years earlier at the Galeries Lafayette in Regent Street. It so happened that she came from this part of the town and I told her about my fiancé and the fact that I had been invited to meet his parents. She answered in the nastiest way: 'You are barking up the wrong tree, my girl. Your fiancé will never marry you. I know his people. They will never allow it.' She added: 'Besides, what would you do with a clergyman's son?' Having been six months at the Savoy, I had travelled a long way since she and I had worked at the Galeries Lafayette. I was no longer the timid salesgirl. I had met millionaires, authors, film producers, newspaper owners and publishers from both sides of the Atlantic. If my former colleague supposed that my fiancé, being the son of a clergyman, was too good for me, I was not entirely convinced that secretly I did not aim higher. And at this precise moment, bearing in mind what

I had just seen of Brentford High Street I could tell myself that in truth there was nothing in the neighbourhood to give it an advantage over the purlieus of Clichy, and that if Hounslow could boast of a highwayman, Clichy could glory in the name of the incomparable Madame de Staël, who was a brilliant enough heroine for any girl, even as ambitious as I was. Thus in my mind, while waiting for the front door to be opened, I sent the image of my former colleague back behind her counter to continue folding her silk stockings at 3s. 9d. a pair or, if one wanted the finer kind, three pairs for a guinea. Now came the sound of quick, light footsteps.

A girl in a white apron opened the door. A dog barked, not loudly, the angry yapping of a lapdog. A pekinese. My future mother-in-law appeared. Tall, slightly bent, white-haired. 'Mother, this is Madeleine,' said my fiancé. This serious, beautiful face under the neat white hair puzzled and fascinated me. I was not accustomed to age. All the women in the world in which I moved were relatively young. My own mother was scarcely twice my age. People took us on occasion for sisters, which because it gave her a flush of pleasure was not of a nature to displease me. My fiancé's mother on the other hand gave me the impression of having stepped down from another century. Her features, though soft, had a Quakerish determination. She was not the sort of woman with whom a girl like myself would have dared take the slightest liberty. I felt extremely impressed, shy but extraordinarily at peace in her presence. However, to give myself confidence I pretended to make a great fuss of her pekinese, which in some curious way seemed by its obvious attachment to her to form a part of herself. I could not guess what a tragic role it was innocently to play in all our lives. This had nothing to do with the fact that as I grew older I also was to own a long line of pekinese, as if I was unconsciously inheriting not only something of the character of the remarkable woman who was to prove my mother-in-law but also that of her gifted female forbears. Thus the tie between mother-in-law and daughter-in-law, occasionally unfortunate, became increasingly blessed and happy, and now that I have reached the age that she then was, I am tempted to say with Ruth and Naomi: 'Entreat me not to leave thee, or to return from following after thee; for whither thou goest, I will go.'

The house proved no less a surprise than my future mother-in-law and her husband, a slightly stout, silent man whose ecclesiastical features and thinning white hair, his clerical suit and collar, caused me to revise my opinion that he would perhaps easily fall before my youthfully feminine charms. I surmised, as indeed proved the case, that if my arrival into the family were to provoke doubts it would be in the mind of this grave and taciturn man rather than in that of his brilliant and erudite wife. I foresaw, for a time at least, a polite coolness.

But to concentrate for a moment on the house. The slope down which Robert and I had come after alighting from the tram had brought us to this handsome entrance that, with its heavy door and twin pillars, still gave no indication of the breathtaking beauty not only of the interior but of the view from all the main rooms, which I have seldom seen equalled for tranquil majesty in any part of the world. My first glimpse of the magnificence of this scene was from the dining-room, with its Jacobean fireplace and green walls on which hung in close proximity paintings in heavy gilt frames. Lunch was laid on a heavy centre table over which was suspended an oil-lamp with a pink shade. Great bay windows against which grew the creeping vine, clusters of grapes half hidden amongst the foliage, looked out on a scene of diversified beauty. First there was the vicar's garden with its ornamental pond, its long bed of lilies of the valley, its immense mulberry tree propped up so old it was, as old as the house itself, its raspberry and loganberry canes, its apple trees and the low wall at the bottom, on the other side of which flowed the Thames. The river itself was here of immense width, divided into channels by the multiplicity of its eyots, some large, some small, on some of which grew willows for the basket-makers, on others tall trees. Along the far bank ran the towing-path that led from Kew to Richmond and beyond that again, like the back-drop of a stage, the giant trees of Kew Gardens, with a glimpse between them of the historic red-bricked Dutch House round which the mad King George chased Fanny Burney.

The nearest arm of the river was separated from the main stream by a very small eyot, amongst the willows of which nested the kingfisher and the swans that belonged to the Crown. These sailed quietly past followed by their cygnets, while up and down the main stream over against Kew Gardens steamed gracefully proportioned tugs drawing behind them as many as eight or ten barges, and now and again noisily hooting, so that the aggressive, melancholy noise reverberated over sparkling water and willow eyot.

All the river noises came in to us through the open windows as we lunched round this table with its simple fare on the white damask cloth. Conversation was doubtless difficult for all of us. Absurdly perhaps the words of a song I had heard as a girl in Paris during the war, in 1916 I think, ran through my head:

> Tout le long de la Tamise
> Ils sont allés tous les deux,
> Goûter l'heure exquise
> Du printemps qui grise.

From time to time, seated between my future mother-in-law and her son, my eyes considered the paintings in their gilt frames on the wall opposite me. My fiancé's mother, intrigued by my obvious interest, said: 'They are by my mother. Amongst her many artistic gifts she was one of the foremost water-colourists of her day and those are copies she made of Old Masters at Florence or at the Prado in Madrid. The olive green of the walls is an ideal background for them.' This was her first mention of the woman who was subsequently to exert by her pictures and her writings so important an influence on my life. But of course I should have known that it was natural that learning to appreciate my future mother-in-law I should learn to admire her mother, for do not daughters live through their mothers, just as I have always lived through mine!

The little maid in her white apron came in with the sweet. I looked from my fiancé's mother to her son. The resemblance was striking, the same vivid blue eyes, soft and laughing, the same slightly prominent nose that gave them determination and character, the same-shaped mouth, the lips thin but by no means cruel though it would not be wise to oppose their will. My

14

mother-in-law in addition had the loveliest hands, and her fingers were covered with those peculiarly Victorian rings in which four or five rubies or emeralds were grouped side by side in heavy gold settings, the gold itself being worked into foliage design so that it had a warmth singularly lacking in the gold or platinum of modern rings. I was soon to learn that all of them had belonged to her mother and most before that to her grandmother, and indeed in all the house there was this continuity through daughter to mother and from mother to grandmother that was to stress its chief characteristic, and make the very idea of entering into it as daughter-in-law something so strangely important. In turn I was to wear several of the rings I saw my mother-in-law wearing at this difficult lunch, one in particular with five sapphires, which alas in due course from continuous wear by successive women of four generations became so thin that the stones had to be reset in the modern way, which robbed them of their beloved individuality.

But one cannot judge the soul of a house by the dining-room alone. Of course, my mother-in-law, as I think of her now, showed me over it. She never treated me otherwise than as a future daughter. Opposite the dining-room, at the foot of the stairs, was her 'Little Room', an intimate feminine sanctum where she worked, a room cluttered with books, papers, heirlooms, photographs and paintings, and whose windows, like those of the dining-room, looked out on the garden and the river, whose noises were so familiar to her that she could tell by the hoot of a tug or the call of a lighterman what message was being relayed. I recall stopping to look at the large framed portrait of a bearded young man wearing the uniform of an officer in the Scots Guards, being struck by the depth of his blue eyes and the rather prominent nose. But the period, because of my inexperience, was difficult to place. At all events, it was not modern, possibly mid-Victorian, and I was about to forget both the portrait and what had struck me as interesting about the features, when my fiancé's mother, who had been watching me, said:

'He was my Uncle Bob, then Colonel Robert Lloyd-Lindsay, V.C., of the Scots Guards, later Lord Wantage. My son is called after him.'

'Oh!' I answered reflectively. 'I often wondered. He tells me so little about himself.'

I would have preferred her to talk about her mother, to whom she had referred on several occasions, especially when discussing the paintings on the walls of the dining-room, as Peli. She pronounced this obviously affectionate nickname as one pronounces the first two syllables of the word Pelican, but whether because of some connection with the 102nd Psalm, or because of Edward Lear's nonsense verses:

Ploffskin, Pluffskin, Pelican jee,
We think no Birds so happy as we!

I had no means to tell. I was too shy to ask a direct question, and so dismissing this detail of mother–daughter relationship, I merely waited for her to tell me more about the Uncle Bob after whom my own Robert was named.

Well, it appeared there had been a General Lindsay who, in 1823, married Anne, the eldest child of Sir Coutts Trotter, the banker, and he took her to the family home of Balcarres in Fifeshire, where she bore him seven children, of whom four survived. Of these the eldest son, Sir Coutts Lindsay, inherited the baronetcy, without assuming the name, of his maternal grandfather, and married Blanche FitzRoy, the woman I wanted to know all about, the Peli of the water-colours in the dining-room. Sir Coutts was himself an artist and painted many portraits of his wife. The General's elder daughter, Margaret, married her cousin, Alexander Lord Lindsay, subsequently twenty-fifth Earl of Crawford. The youngest son, Robert, in front of whose portrait we were standing, won his V.C. while defending the Queen's colours during the Battle of Alma, and subsequently became Lord Wantage. He married Harriet, the only child of the wealthy banker Lord Overstone—'my Aunt Harriet', said my mother-in-law, as she showed me a picture which now hangs in the low room of my farmhouse.

I was later on many occasions to remain with my fiancé's mother in what everybody called her 'little room', and I shall have occasion to describe it in greater detail. She took me

16

upstairs to what was known as the schoolroom, which had the same magnificent view as the dining-room. There was a tall fender against the black coal-fire grate, a plain deal table and a wall covered with bookshelves, in which there was the entire series of coloured fairy-books edited by Andrew Lang which a Rothschild cousin had given Robert as a childhood present; *Les Malheurs de Sophie* and all the other works of the Comtesse de Ségur, which were delightfully familiar to me; and a profusion of books that English children read before 1914 such as *She* and *Allan Quartermain* by Rider Haggard, *Kenilworth* and *Ivanhoe* by Sir Walter Scott, *Kidnapped*, *The Master of Ballantrae* and *Treasure Island* by Stevenson, the Ballads of Kipling and so on. At the plain deal table in the middle of the room, my future mother-in-law explained, her son and her elder daughter, Katherine, had lessons every morning until they were of school age from a French governess who had become known as Mallalal. She arrived punctually at 9 a.m., took off her hat and veil, opened the proceedings by making the children read a chapter from the New Testament in French aloud, after which they settled down to dictation, history and arithmetic. At midday she would take them for a walk along the High Street, past Kew Bridge and generally as far as Gunnersbury underground station, beside which there was a small haberdasher's where she bought gloves, ribbons and sewing-cotton. They would be back in time for the two children to wash their hands and get ready for one o'clock lunch in the dining-room in which we had just lunched, where they would normally meet the vicar and herself for the first time in the day. After lunch, Mademoiselle would return to town and the children would be taken to spend the afternoon at Gunnersbury Park, the Rothschild estate between Kew Bridge and Acton, less than half a mile away. Their companion on these expeditions had been a succession of German girls whom my future mother-in-law engaged in order that her children should learn to speak German as fluently as they spoke French with Mademoiselle in the morning. As few of the German girls spoke English the two children had no alternative but to speak German with her during the half-mile walk to and from the park. Once there, of course, they were free to play by themselves, exploring the woods, the

17

orchards, the lake with its many-coloured ducks and geese, its primrose-covered banks and grotto, in which there was always a rowboat.

'When my son went to Eton and his sister to St Paul's all this came to an end,' said my future mother-in-law, 'but those lessons from a French governess every morning may well have predisposed my son into falling in love with you.'

We were standing by this table where Robert had learnt to write and to read, but I felt singularly inane and began to tell my fiancé's mother that before leaving home I had washed my hair in her honour and that it would not curl. She appeared surprised to have been let into this feminine secret but her expression changed, and for the first time she gave me a sweetly affectionate smile. Something was beginning to tell me that in spite of disappointment, especially at the vicar's coolness, a secret link was being forged between daughter-in-law and mother-in-law and everything would be all right. In spite of this the ordeal of tea was to mark the low point of my inept behaviour. The vicar emerged from his study, a large and beautiful room that may well have been added to the house in early Georgian times. It had the same sweeping view across garden and river but it was on a slightly lower level, the equivalent of five or six steps. Here, according to Victorian custom, the vicar held morning prayers at which the maids were present. At 10 a.m. he received the church officials, the district nurses and all those who sought an audience. He wrote his sermons here, slept for half an hour with a knotted handkerchief over his face after lunch, worked until tea-time and, after supper, the family met there to spend the evening.

My future mother-in-law served me with China tea and I had difficulty pretending that I liked it. The little maid came in and out with hot buttered toast and thinly cut bread and butter. She gave me quick sideway glances and I wondered if I ought to respond. We must have been about the same age and I envied her for appearing to be so much at home in this house which continued to terrify me. After the bread and butter she brought in the evening paper and set it before the vicar. It was the *Evening News* and I was not then to know what an immensely important role that newspaper was soon to play in my young married life. My throat was dry and I could eat nothing. The vicar called his wife Effie, which was short for Euphemia, and she called him Burr. We had been sitting round the table; now she got up and took me over to the window. By the low wall at the foot of the garden, in the narrow channel between the bulrushes and the eyot, there was a dock for the mending of barges, and all day there arose from it a symphony of men's voices and incessant hammering. Though one might have supposed that this noise could quickly become irksome in fact it was not, making only background music for the hooting of the tugs, the lapping of water, the call of birds. The scene was one of continual movement, tugs passing distantly at what seemed to be surprising speed, making their way to West-minster Bridge, the Embankment, the Tower of London and the river mouth, where they would meet the big ships from all over the world. A cat clambered up the vine and looked in at the window beside which we were standing. It opened its mouth and miaowed but as the window was closed we heard nothing. My fiancé's mother smiled. She said that this was the first cat for which she had anything like affection. Normally, because her mother, Peli, had liked them, she confined her affection for animals to pekinese, but the particular pekinese I had made such a fuss of before lunch was showing a tendency to prefer the vicar. Could it be that my future mother-in-law disliked shared loyal-ties? My deplorable silences at the tea-table provoked me to exclaim that my mother and I also owned a cat and that its name was Nanny, and that one of the reasons for which I was so happy to have made my home in England was that, as everybody knows, English people love animals. At this point, aware that my outburst had proved even more ridiculous than my silences, I became dumb again and felt the blood rushing up to my hair-line.

Fortunately it was time for Robert and me to go back to town.

The heavy tram rattled noisily along the High Street on its way to Kew Bridge. 'I wish I hadn't come,' I said. 'I made a dreadful fool of myself. And why on earth did I have to tell your mother that I had washed my hair in her honour! She must have thought me crazy.'

'That's my father's church,' he said, pointing out of the window. 'It's called St George's. My father is very proud that his church is named after the patron saint of England.'

'I saw the church on our way to lunch,' I said, 'and you needn't rub it in that your father dislikes everything that isn't English. His attitude is all too apparent.'

Silence.

'Why did you never mention the V.C. after whom you are called?' I asked. 'What was he like?'

'I have no idea,' he said. 'He died in the year in which I was born. On the other hand my Aunt Harriet was a formidable figure with whom I was sent to stay when I was eight or nine. At the time of her marriage to my Uncle Bob, her father, the banker Lord Overstone, settled on them not only the major part of his vast fortune but also all his extensive landed estates in Berkshire. The house was called Lockinge and I was so impressed by its magnificence, my aunt herself with her black lace, her pearls and emeralds, her matriarchal features, mittened hands and ebony stick, and the liveried servants who busied themselves bringing logs for the fire in the great hall, that I persisted in calling her Lady Wantage. Her anger made me feel miserable. Well, that's about all except that there was a trout stream running through the lawns in front of the house and that all the meadows were filled with cowslips. I wish I could tell you more but I seem to have gone through my youth missing opportunities. As for Aunt Harriet, she was like all the women in my mother's family. They painted pictures, wrote books, administered vast estates. All of them left big names.'

'I understand why my arrival brings sorrow,' I said.

'Who can tell?' he answered.

We dined at the Ivy that evening and neither of us made any further mention of our visit to Brentford. The question of our respective families did not weigh with us when we found ourselves contentedly alone. But when in due course I was back at home with my mother she interpreted my awkward silences as an admission of defeat. After all, she had been waiting anxiously all day for news.

'I warned you,' she said after a while. 'I sensed that you would be wasting your time.'

I winced. She was by nature deeply suspicious. She was eternally putting me on my guard. A girl alone, or nearly alone, in a great city is at the mercy of so many dangers. Maternal love filled her with ambition for me but experience told her that life is full of pitfalls for girls who have only their youth to offer. Under my mother's influence we passed from hope to dismay at the drop of a word. My silence tortured her but how was I to explain, without hurting her feelings, the things I had seen or heard? How was I to tell her about Effie's Little Room, about the Dowager with the black lace and the mittens who administered great tracts of Berkshire downs, a house with logs burning in a great hall, a trout stream in the garden and fields full of cowslips? 'You must have had a dreadful time,' she said. 'And I feel sorry for your young man. You have put him in a ridiculous position. You're much too young and flippant to understand. Your silly head is full of pretty clothes and the latest dance step. You are utterly selfish, like all girls of your generation, who think that as soon as they appear on the scene the world will fall at their feet. But those old English families are like fortified castles. A poor girl doesn't easily take them by assault.'

Yes, but I had a ring on the right finger—a deep blue sapphire solitaire from the firm of Lacloche in Bond Street. Robert had wanted to give me an emerald and had indeed chosen it, but when the stone was sent to Paris for setting it was unaccountably lost in the post—a story that for several weeks, until confirmed to me personally by the jeweller, I had refused to believe. In order to waste no further time, Robert chose the sapphire, a stone already set. At about this time he was sent to Geneva by the *Morning Post* in order to cover some conference. Before leaving London he had brought me a Memoir of Uncle Bob by his widow, in which she had written on the fly-leaf: 'To Bobbie Henrey from his affectionate Aunt and Godmother—Harriet Wantage. Lockinge, May 1913.' He brought me at the same time an invitation from his mother to spend a night at Brentford during his absence.

That evening on opening the volume I discovered a reproduction of the portrait I had seen in my future mother-in-law's

Little Room of the young bearded officer, and turning the pages,
I read:

'His father, General Lindsay, had an interview later on with the
Duke of Cambridge, after his return from the Crimea, who said:
"I can tell you, General, your son is a very fine fellow, a most
gallant soldier among gallant men, for they are a most noble set of
fellows. How he escaped has been a marvel to me. I watched him
carrying the Queen's colours at Alma—at one moment I thought
him gone, the colours fell and he disappeared under them, but
presently he came out from below them, the flagstaff had been
cut and the colours fell over him, but he raised them again and
waved them over his head. He has my highest approbation."'

Aunt Harriet added that thirty-four years later, in the autumn of
1888, her husband took her to walk over the field of Alma and as
the scenes of the battle came back into his mind, he said to her:
'The Brigade of Guards had not previously been opposite to an
enemy in the field since the Battle of Waterloo. Two of our officers
who had seen active service became on the morning of the battle
quite authorities. Berkeley had been in the Cape war, and
Annesley, who was one of his junior ensigns, had a great deal to
say. When the first shot was fired he drew his watch from his
pocket and said with a magnificent air: "The battle begins at
one o'clock." His sangfroid at the time made an impression on
me. Poor fellow, he came out of the engagement with only one
tooth left in his head, but I meet him now in the House of Lords,
and his face shows no sign of the frightful wound he sustained.
. . . The duty of carrying the colours is performed by the junior
ensign while on the march, but in action the colours are carried by
the senior subaltern. I being senior, carried the Queen's colours,
and Thistlethwayte, coming next, carried the regimental colours.
. . . The colours I carried were shot through in a dozen places,
and the colour-staff was cut in two. My great object was to plant
the standard on the Russian redoubt, and my impression is that
nobody was into the earthworks before I was.'

Uncle Bob had married Aunt Harriet in 1858 at St Martin-in-
the-Fields, and Lloyd-Lindsay, as he was then, aged only twenty-

seven, left the Army with the rank of lieutenant-colonel, to live with his young wife at Lockinge on the 20,000 acres Berkshire estate that Lord Overstone had settled on his daughter at the time of the marriage. But it was not immediately a total abandonment of travel abroad. The war that broke out between Germany and France in 1870 drew the young colonel temporarily away from his farms. The Swiss had taken the lead in Red Cross work abroad, and the Geneva Conference had led to the formation of Red Cross societies almost everywhere except in England. Uncle Bob boldly took the lead and within a week of the outbreak of war wrote to *The Times* suggesting the formation of a society of which he was immediately afterwards elected chairman—Queen Victoria being patroness. On the board were the Earl of Shaftesbury, Lord Overstone, Baron N. de Rothschild and Viscount Bury, who had been a brother officer of Uncle Bob in the Crimea. Money was quickly and easily raised, and the Committee divided equally between the French and German armies a sum of £40,000 to relieve the sick and wounded of the two armies. Uncle Bob undertook the duty of conveying this sum in person, and accordingly set out for the German headquarters at Versailles. For by now things had moved so quickly that the Siege of Paris had begun. He set out by way of Rouen, reached Versailles on 9th October, lunched with the Crown Prince and Bismarck and a few days later dined with the King of Prussia, who gave him the impression of a bluff, good-natured, outspoken old soldier, though he seemed a little huffy at the proposed division of the money between his wounded and the French, saying: 'You certainly are very impartial, indeed!' Afterwards he spent an hour with Bismarck in his private room, smoking cigars and talking freely and openly upon many subjects. 'I never saw a man who gives at once so strong an impression of commanding talent and intense determination and energy; his figure is gigantic and magnificent, the face plain; thick, shaggy white eyebrows, cheeks baggy under the eyes, but a fine profile and a grand shaped massive head, well placed upon powerful shoulders. He spoke to me about the Lindsays, saying they were a fine family, and had played a great part in Scottish history.'

Bismarck gave him letters and an escort to enter Paris. A

lieutenant of Hessian infantry accompanied his servant and himself as far as Ville d'Avray, at which point he was handed over to the colonel of the regiment occupying the village. From here a young lieutenant of Hussars rode beside Uncle Bob's carriage to the outpost near the old porcelain manufactory in the village of Sèvres. He was then ordered to leave the carriage and, preceded by a trumpeter on horseback with a white flag fastened on his sword, and accompanied by an officer also on horseback, Uncle Bob and his servant, Whittle, carrying a bag and a Red Cross flag, marched in silence to the barricade at the end of the deserted street. Here they halted and the trumpeter sounded a blast and waved his white flag. After about an hour, the two Englishmen crossed the river in a small boat and walked to the headquarters of the general commanding the outpost in the village of Boulogne. A carriage was provided for them by the French and they drove through the Bois de Boulogne, down the Champs Elysées and to the Palace of the Louvre where later Uncle Bob had an interview with General Trochu.

Though Uncle Bob's sympathy might well have leant gently towards the German side, I had been struck since first meeting Robert's family, and more especially his mother, by the way in which French influence or the language was never far distant. My fiancé, through those childhood lessons every morning from a French governess at the schoolroom table at Brentford, was perfectly at home in the two languages. Uncle Bob had fought beside the French in the Crimea, and an exquisite picture by Sir John Millais that hung in Robert's room at Brentford showed his mother 'Effie' as a little girl of four (the artist dated the picture 1869) kneeling in front of her old French nurse who is holding an open picture-book on her voluminous knees. It is true, of course, that the German influence was never far away and that Effie, in addition to all this, was accustomed to read the New Testament both in the Latin Vulgate and in Greek, but that was not so unusual in women of superior intelligence educated by governesses at home. At all events with her I never had a feeling of being foreign. Indeed everybody in the house except Burr was, to say the least, more or less bilingual, and by this time I who

24

had come to the country so young felt myself by love and adoption as much English as French. I was aware, of course, that for the moment my knowledge about Effie and her forbears was slight, but I felt confident that gradually I would glean from her in the course of intimate mother-in-law daughter-in-law feminine conversations everything I wanted to know. As for being put off by the idea of some immense, frightening discrepancy in fortune, I never allowed it to worry me. The vicarage gave no sign of lacking anything essential but on the other hand, except in charity, my future mother-in-law gave the impression of counting her pennies. Yes, of course, there had been Uncle Robert but he had died before I was born, and though I had seen a letter of his quoted in the Memoir and dated 1895: 'I am now, and have been for some time, probably the largest farmer in England . . .' (no wonder, with over 20,000 acres!) my fiancé had assured me that none of his fortune, or Aunt Harriet's, had come to them,—and as for the vicar's stipend, believe it or not, it had never exceeded £400 a year!

But maybe I had convinced myself too quickly that the walls of the castle had fallen. The evening I arrived to stay the house was not particularly welcoming, and I was obliged to make my usual fuss of the pekinese, which was old, bloodshot of eye and often evil-smelling. However, he seemed to understand that I was unhappy and that we could join our relative miseries. I now made an amazing discovery. Except for a very inefficient jet in my future father-in-law's study the house continued as in Victorian times to rely on oil-lamps and candles. Incredible as it may seem, at bedtime we each took up a lighted candle and marched up to our rooms, while the vicar rattled his safe to see that it was properly closed and Effie inspected the locks and chains of the front door. I had never experienced anything quite like this. Until he had more or less left home to work in London, Robert had slept in a lovely room next to that of his parents at the top of the stairs opposite the old schoolroom. From his bed he could see the lights of the tugs as they made their way to the Tower of London and the docks. Men's voices floated across the darkened river and owls in the tall trees which separated the vicar's garden from the brewery. In summer when Effie gave her garden parties for the members of her Mothers' Meeting, Chinese lanterns were suspended across the ornamental pond and the brass band from the gasworks played valses while Mr Stamp the churchwarden's two girls, Alice and Dorothy, handed round strawberries and cream. But during the war these festivities had been abandoned and then the night sky was lit up with dozens of searchlights trying to capture a zeppelin in their beams.

This room was now used by the vicar as a dressing-room and Robert, perhaps as a punishment for leaving home, had been relegated to a small room at the back of the house whose window overlooked the slope and the iron gate leading to the High Street. It was a damp, dreary, sparsely furnished room with an iron bedstead and the most uncomfortable springs I had ever tried to sleep on. The noise of the heavy tramcars clanging up and down the High Street between Hounslow and Hampton Court and Shepherd's Bush and Hammersmith did not cease till well after midnight. This was the room that in his youth had been occupied by the various German maids who took the children to Gunnersbury Park in the afternoon—and once or twice there had been a Russian girl whose parents sent her letters with small Russian stamps on the envelopes bearing the emblem of the Czars, and which she would give the vicar for his stamp collection. What loneliness must have been shut up and preserved within these dreary walls. What affinity I felt with the poor little Russian girls so far from home, the little German girls who succeeded one another for a wage of £18 a year—and a present of three yards of horrible dress material at Christmas! My candle in its tin socket spluttered and ran. When I tried to snuff it, hot wax burnt my fingers. Robert had stacked a number of French yellow-back novels on a chest of drawers. They had been sent to him by Marie-Laure Bischoffsheim, heiress to an immense fortune, who was to become Vicomtesse de Noailles and whom he met at Oxford. Francis de Croisset, the playwright, was her stepfather and she knew all the great writers like Marcel Proust in Paris, who sent her their inscribed books. We brought the entire bundle later to our apartment in Brompton Road and they were to form part of my young-wifely education.

I picked up a book but could not concentrate. I took up another one. It was called *Green Leaves*. Small, square and slim, it had a green cover and little leaves embossed in gold leaf framing the title. The author's name did not appear on the cover or on the spine. One had to look inside. The volume consisted of quarterly leaflets written by Lady Lindsay, who was the Peli of the water-colours on the dining-room walls. I had discovered something infinitely precious.

The title was repeated on the first page of each pamphlet, with the following quotation from Ecclesiasticus xiv 18: 'As of the green leaves on a thick tree, some fall, and some grow' and the first was dated April 1903. Here and there as I turned the pages by the light of my single candle, I discovered scattered, disjointed memories of this Blanche FitzRoy who grew up to be the inspiration of the Pre-Raphaelites, who founded the Grosvenor Gallery that was to make history, who travelled in Italy with the Brownings, who was sung by Gilbert and Sullivan in *Patience*, who accompanied Melba on her Stradivarius violin, was a water-colourist admired by Tennyson and was painted playing the violin in his most famous portrait by G. F. Watts—writer, novelist—and who married Uncle Bob's elder brother, Sir Coutts Lindsay, soldier turned artist whose pictures (many of them portraits of Blanche) were to be found, together with those of his wife, on the walls of this hidden vicarage nestling so unexpectedly between clanging High Street and swiftly running river.

This is what I found in the book: 'Autumn seems to be specially the time for memories. Green leaves are sere upon bush and tree; a few roses linger feebly on the garden wall among chrysanthemums and reddened creepers. Days shorten rapidly'.

On another page Blanche Lindsey reflected: 'What is my earliest recollection?' Well, perhaps, the visit to a country fair in Norfolk; I was taken thither in a green painted go-cart drawn by my father and mother alternately. How vividly I remember the scene! The crowd, the greasy pole decked at the top with gaily coloured ribbon streamers and a leg of mutton—the prize for the successful climber. Somewhat later—I was four years old— a clear incident is the journey to Pau, partly in a *diligence* (or stage coach), the *intérieur*, or centre, of which was given up to my brother, myself, and our French nurse; then the *Parc* at Pau, where we played with hoops—mine was adorned with red velvet and gilt bells—in sight of the beautiful snow-capped mountains of the Pyrenees which I loved. And what of mental teaching? First, never to omit daily prayer, morning and evening, however short. Next, not to forget that for an English girl it would be absolutely dishonourable to tell a lie. One very hot day at Tunbridge Wells when I was six, I sat alone under the trees reading a favourite book called *Pleasant Pages*. I came upon a saying which I have not since seen in print. "Write injuries in dust, and kindness in marble." This impressed me so much that I forthwith indited various girlish grievances in the dusty road with the aid of a stick, pausing to watch the light wind obliterate the words, and feeling much exhilarated by the performance.

'Is it worth while to recall such slight memories of one's girlhood? Yes, perhaps if things change sufficiently to cause surprise by contrast. If we converse with really old people, and travel back, so to speak, on their memories, what a long way we can go! And how strange their comportment sometimes seems to us. I knew an old lady who lived when she was young at the beginning of the 19th century, at Edinburgh, at a time when, owing to its literary and artistic activity, the northern city was called the Modern Athens. She had also often been the guest of Wordsworth in his lake-country home.

'Again in my girlhood, I met at Paris an old Mademoiselle who clearly remembered the horrors of the great French Revolution of 1789. Old people whom the sorrows and struggles of life have left calm and large-minded, and who are kindly disposed toward the young, are truly attractive and interesting.

'Which does not mean that as a girl, my thoughts were exclusively turned to the past. Far from that, I burned with eagerness to discover the wonders and excitement of young womanhood, and as it was the habit amongst girls of my generation, to put many of their thoughts into verse, I wrote these lines which I later included in a volume for children called *A String of Beads*.

A little girl was sitting
Alone beneath the trees,
And her thoughts were floating onward
Beyond the purple seas,
Beyond the streak of purple hill,
Beyond the distance fair,
To the dim land of the Future
And its castle in the air.

Her hands were folded idly,
Her blue eyes filled with tears,
As she thought 'How far the future,
And how long my childish years!
For were I grown up, surely
The world might scarcely hold
The boundless joy of each bright day;
Ah, could I but grow old!'

'As a very young woman, I made the acquaintance of General Sir Hope Grant, who was then already old. He was interested in me because my home was where his only sister had lived and died. His military fame makes it unnecessary for me to describe his active career. He had an intense love for his old regiment, the 9th Lancers. A look of affection came into his face whenever he mentioned it. He did not willingly speak of his soldier life, nor of any of the fighting he had witnessed, or the dangers he had been in. Above all, he could not bear to speak of the Indian Mutiny. However, when I pressed him hard to tell me his most terrible experience, he answered that it was at Cawnpore, on the day that the English neared that fearful and historic well, filled with its hapless victims. He had been totally unprepared for the ghastly sight. The day was beautiful, the sun was shining hotly; the grass was green around the well, and on the grass he espied something white; he stooped to pick it up—it was the tiny hand of an English baby. His men were maddened and could not be restrained; indeed the appalling sight of the well at Cawnpore changed many merciful kind-hearted fellows into pitiless avengers, for the time being at least. Sir Hope died in London.

'On the day of his death, he asked me to go and see him. He said farewell to several of his friends. When I arrived, only Lady Grant was present, though a short time previously the Prince of Wales had been sitting with him. He talked resignedly, even happily, of his coming end, and of various friends and earthly interests. Then, when I was about to leave him, he sat up in bed, his dark eyes more eager than ever, and he stretched forward and grasped my hand in both of his: "I am dying, dear Lady Lindsay," he said. "Do not forget what I say: love the Lord Jesus Christ—that is the only thing worth living for."

'When I was a small girl, I remember often going out with my father in the "cab", or hooded cabriolet, which he drove himself, a groom standing up behind after the fashion of the time. One day our horse became restive, and kicked and plunged, so that the vehicle was smashed to pieces. My father lifted me out, and placing me on a bank close to the road, bade me sit there quietly. Quietly I sat, weeping silently nevertheless. Then the old retriever, Sambo, came to me, and put one heavy paw on my lap, wishing as plainly as possible to say: "Don't be frightened!"

'I was greatly pleased by the story of the king who searched far and wide through his dominions to find a really contented man. An oracle had assured the king that if he could but obtain the shirt of a perfectly contented man and wear it, he himself would become contented and happy. His messengers scoured the country; finally after innumerable efforts in every direction, an absolutely happy man was found. Alas! he was a beggar; utterly destitute. He wore no shirt!

'In the French language, "être content" means to be happy, joyful, not merely contented or tolerably satisfied. The scene where I first heard, and indeed was made to write out the above story, and thus perhaps impress it indelibly on my mind—that scene of long years ago rises up before me. My young seventeen years old French governess (a professor's daughter) and I, a girl of eleven, were "doing lessons" in my schoolroom at Tours, while from the window was a delightful view of the next door confectioner preparing elaborate cakes, which were to be later on, in the front shop, the delight and envy of all passers-by. "Contentment", she adds, quoting from an old calendar on her desk, "swells a Mite into a Talent, and makes a man richer than the Indies." ' She goes on:

'Not long ago I was sorting some papers in an old despatch case that had belonged to my father. I came upon a very curious scarf-pin. The small stone or ivory in the centre of it—white and long-shaped—was set in gold. Suddenly, a recollection flashed into my mind. I was a tiny girl again, and my father was saying to me: "Two-shoes, if you have that eye-tooth out tomorrow without a sob or a cry, I will promise to have it mounted and to wear it as a pin." Being possessed of only the slenderest courage, I suppose that my love for my father kept me silent and tearless during the operation. Be that as it may, I well recollect his wearing it as he walked up and down the Marine Parade at Brighton. Poor little pin! It must have provoked some strange comments, smiling questions, perhaps. Anyhow, I was proud enough of it then and as, after many, many years I gazed upon it instantly my eyes grew dim, and I thought lovingly of the fatherly love that had prompted the little episode.

'When I was a little girl, I was once admitted to an old gentleman's lovely garden near Slough, and there given permission to pick one flower, the one I should prefer. For some undefined reason—incomprehensible to everyone but my girlish self, and difficult for this older self nowadays to appreciate—I selected a somewhat colourless and of course non-fragrant Sweet William. I remember vividly my mother's questioning: "Why did you not choose a rose?" I can see the furtive smiles of other people who were present; the kind owner himself looked amused, whilst ordering for me at his gardener's hands a bounteous bunch of roses. Nay, I can never, even now, see the flower called Sweet William, without a sudden touch of shyness and shame of that hour of my girlhood. And yet I read in Gerarde's Herbal (dated 1597) the following praise of Sweet Williams: "These plants are not used either in meat or in medicine, but esteemed for their beauty to decke up gardens, the bodices of the beautifull.'

'Not long ago I was in an Italian town, San Giminiano, where the memory of a little peasant girl, who lived in the fourteenth century, is still reverenced as that of a saint. Poor little Fina was condemned at ten years of age to absolute inaction owing to an incurable disease. Therefore she chose, through the five remaining years of her life, to lie comfortless on a hard board, in order to share, as far as possible, the sufferings of our Lord. Her resolution reminded me of the fortitude of a modern English girl. I have before me a short memoir of Laura FitzRoy, my father's sister, who, in days before the discovery of anaesthetics, endured a terrible operation with almost incredible courage, when only thirteen years of age. My aunt, Lady Southampton, has allowed me to copy the following letter addressed to her by the Reverend W. H. Langhorne of Worton Rectory, Oxford, who quotes from an album which belonged to his mother:

"Clifton, 10th April 1819. Our circle here has been, during the last week, greatly interested by the very affecting circumstances which have occurred regarding little Laura FitzRoy, Lady Southampton's second daughter. She was attacked with a white swelling on her knee some time ago. Every human effort made to remove it proved ineffectual, and a surgeon from London came down here for consultation, who at last decided that nothing could save her life but amputation. Lady Southampton was at first quite overwhelmed with the thought of her child enduring such torture, and replied that she could not bring her mind to consent to it, and felt as if she could more easily part with her entirely than to expose her to such suffering. This afflicting conflict lasted for some days when, divinely supported, her will was lost in the will of God, and her consent was fully given. Mr Baynton, the surgeon here, a man of remarkably benevolent feelings, said he really could not undertake to apprise the dear girl of the sad alternative. 'No,' her mother replied; she would undertake that herself, and was enabled to do it with the utmost unlooked-for calmness and composure.

"After addressing Laura in the most affectionate manner, she told her that to suffer amputation was the only manner left to save her life. Laura heard her without the least agitation, and replied, 'God demands my limb but not my life.'

'Do you think me unkind, my love, to have made such a decision?'

'Oh, no, Mamma! What else could you have done? You know you have tried everything.'

'If you had it in your choice, would you prefer to die, as you must do if this operation is not performed?'

'Oh! to die, to be sure, Mamma; for then I am sure I should be happy; but then, you know, that would be taking my life into my own hands, and I could not expect God to support me on my death-bed, nor could I think that, when suffering this, I may be made to glorify God by being of use to Mr Baynton. I hope He will support me through it. Had this happened some time ago Mamma, I was not sure of going to heaven; but do you remember staying one Sunday from church, and conversing a great deal with me about God, saying: "My dear Laura, if you are so impatient under illness it may lead God to afflict you more?" Since then, Mamma, I have thought a great deal more about God. I like always to have you, and I should like to have you in the room with me at the time of the operation. But then, Mamma, you must not, for it would do you harm; I would like to have Bird (the housekeeper) with me if it will not hurt her.' This heavenly state of calmness was no sudden impulse, but every time Lady Southampton returned to her room during the day she found Laura's mind in the same delightful frame.

"Next morning about eleven the surgeons arrived, and Lady Southampton went in to Laura to acquaint her that it was fixed for that day. On hearing that it was so near the tears rolled down her cheeks, and she said, 'Oh, Mamma pray for me! I hope God will support me.' Her former calmness soon returned, and she was taken out of her bed like a lamb without the least agitation or fear expressed. When they wished to put a bandage on her eyes, she said: 'Oh, you need not. I'll shut my eyes; but if you wish it, you may do it,' and they put on the handkerchief. She held a little nosegay between her finger and thumb when taken out of bed, and there it remained until the end of the operation, so still was her whole body. Not a scream was uttered but one during the time. Towards the close, Baynton was praising her fortitude, and she replied: 'Don't praise me, there should not even have been that oh!' She told Mr Baynton that two texts which had supported her during the operation were: "Through much tribulation must we enter into the kingdom of heaven,"; "If we suffer with Him we shall also reign with Him," adding: 'I am so happy that it happened this week (Passion week); it makes me feel as if suffering with Christ.'

"Emily saw her four days ago, and found her in bed eating an orange, and altogether with so much simplicity as if nothing had happened to call forth commendation in any way. She remarked: 'I am so happy in my sick bed. I would not for the world have my leg back again, for you know it is better to enter life halt and maimed than, having two legs, to enter into hell fire.'

"I saw Laura some months ago, and so extremely volatile was she that Lady Southampton almost despaired of making any religious impression on her mind; but she has been the child of much prayer, and much graciously answered prayer, as this detail evinces."

Blanche Lindsay added:

'Laura died in December 1819, a few months after the operation.'

The trams continued at uneven intervals to clatter past the iron gate at the top of the slope. They had the most infuriating way of sounding their strident warning bells. The vicar's cuckoo clock, brought back from a journey to the Matterhorn, hanging over a landing on the stairs, struck, and a sudden uproar in the street, coming to me dimly through the acacia trees on either side of the slope, told me that it was closing time for the pubs at the corner of Ealing Road. Drunken songs and men's deep voices rent the air. It was just like Stacey Street but worse. I was shivering in a crêpe-de-chine nightdress, huddled up in the world's most uncomfortable bed whose springs creaked, as if unoiled, every time I moved. My candle lit up nothing pretty and only half the page I was trying to read. Where did the little maid sleep? Could her room be more dismal than mine? And where did cook sleep? Did they perhaps share a room? How did they keep themselves warm? Were there mice? That would be the end of everything. Nothing could cure me of shrieking when I saw a mouse. Not even Robert when on occasion he had tried to shake me or even slap my face. Mice were an obsession. I saw them climbing up my stockings, under my skirt. Effie and the vicar would doubtless, coming from along the passage in their night attire, think I had gone mad. Suppose I failed to wake up in time for breakfast. Where did they serve breakfast? And at what time? Suppose also that I did not have time to do my hair? Effie wore real tortoise-shell combs in her silky white hair and was always losing them. I had picked one up and exclaimed at the beauty of it. Everything she wore was so delightfully real. Real emeralds on her fingers, real pearls round her neck, real tortoise-shell combs.

I was all nerves and the best was to go on reading a little. I felt like a girl trying to fit together the pieces in a jigsaw puzzle. Who was Blanche? What was she? I mean, who were *her* parents? These glimpses of her girlhood left so many questions un-answered. However, let us turn the page.

'Hans Christian Andersen,' wrote Lady Lindsay in her December 1904 letter, 'has given in *What the Moon Saw* an interesting account of the mother of five sons, who were respectively the founders of the house of Rothschild in different cities of Europe. She lived to be ninety-nine. She was my great grandmother; my mother's grandmother.'

Was Blanche Lindsay, by this revelation, about to answer my silent query?

' "I will now give you a picture from Frankfurt," said the moon. "I especially noticed one building there. It was a private house, plain in appearance, and painted green. It stood near the ancient Jews' street, or Judengasse. It was Rothschild's house. I looked through the open door. The staircase was brilliantly lighted; servants carrying wax candles in massive silver candle-sticks stood there, and bowed low before an aged woman, who was being brought downstairs in a litter. The proprietor of the house stood bareheaded, and repectfully imprinted a kiss on her hand. She was his mother. She nodded in a friendly manner to him and to the servants, and they carried her to the dark, narrow street (the Judengasse), into a little house that was her dwelling. Here her children had been born, from hence the fortune of the family had arisen. If she deserted the despised street and the little house, fortune would also desert her children. That was her firm belief.

'The moon told no more. But I thought of the old woman in the narrow, despised street. A word, and a brilliant house would have arisen for her on the banks of the Thames—a word, and a villa would have been prepared for her by the Bay of Naples. "If I should desert the lowly house, where the fortunes of my sons first began to bloom, fortune would desert them!" It was a superstition of such a class that he who knows the story, and has seen this picture need have only two words placed under the picture to make him understand it; and these two words are: "A mother!"'

Of one of the descendants of this old lady, Blanche Lindsay wrote a little further on:

'In the park at Waddesdon, my cousin, the late Baron Ferdinand Rothschild, showed me one day various pets that came running up to nibble bread from his hand. Amongst others were two sheep which the monks of Mount Athos had given him for food when he was yachting near their monastery. But my cousin had preferred to keep the sheep on his yacht and tame them.'

Effie must have given me somebody else's candle-end for soon there would be nothing left of it, and it would splutter out, leaving me in darkness. Did she perhaps give me Robert's because I was occupying his room?

> The Lanthorn is to keep the Candle Light,
> When it is windy, and a darksome night.

quoted Blanche Lindsay, and she went on to say:

'Joyful it is to a traveller, hurrying along her weary path in murky twilight, to hail the friendly spark of a cottage window, whilst the constellation of twinkling lights of some far-off town speak to her of hope and warmth and comfort. Journeying by carriage in former days over Swiss mountain passes, before tunnels had been pierced for railways, and our tired horses plodded slowly on the upward road, how pleasant it was, when arrived at the summit, suddenly at a happy turn of the route, to espy the small group of flashing lights down in the valley where we were to find food and rest. Ah, then! the driver woke up to immediate cheerfulness, and cracked his whip, inciting his horses by voice and rein. Then indeed the poor animals, who had assuredly like himself caught the promise of a familiar stable, galloped joyfully down the road, perhaps a trifle too joyfully for our nerves as they turned sharp corners above many an alarming precipice!'

Was this an echo of her journeys to Italy with the Brownings? At last my eyes were closing, but would I sleep on this hard bed? Blanche Lindsay appeared to echo my thoughts. She wrote:

'For what would be bed without sleep but a wearisome place wherein we toss and groan, bemoaning our lot, and sighing for the dawn? Sleep is, or should be, a knot of peace, a baiting-place or hostelry; there the traveller seeks rest and peace. I possess a small volume, bearing the date of 1581 and entitled thus: "The Frenche Littleton, a most easie, perfect, and absolute way to learn the frenche tongue: Set forth by Claudias Hollyband." The student is here instructed by a not unusual method of useful conversations, a whole chapter devoted to travellers arriving at an inn.

' "I pray you lead me to the next village," says the traveller, "and I will give you a farthing and I will make you drinke well when we be there arrived. Have we not theeves at the forest? for that troubleth my braines." "No, sir," replies the guide cheerfully; "for the knight marshall hange th'other daye one halfe dosen at the highe tree, at the gibbet which you see afore you, at the top of the mountain." Nevertheless the timid traveller continues: "Truly I feare least we be here robbed," and he continues energetically in the French tongue: "Certes jé peur que nous soyong icy destroussey, devalizey, assassinez, vollez." But the answer is essentially consoling: "No, no, feare not: all the theeves be at the warres." '

As the candle finally spluttered out, I read:

'I knew a Scots lady of great age, Lady Ruthven, who was utterly deaf and nearly blind. She knew the whole book of the Psalms by heart, and recited them steadily to herself in wakeful pauses of the night.'

2

A GIRL AT TWENTY ENDS by sleeping on the hardest bed. The next morning I woke to see the young maid in her white apron holding out a cup of tea. 'It's eight o'clock, Miss,' she said, 'and breakfast is at nine.'

Her eyes had a gleam of amused understanding, and for the first time I smiled back at her. After all we were more or less of the same age. As soon as she had gone I looked slowly round the room, wondering if I had misjudged it, but it struck me as being even more dreary by morning light than by candle-light. The furniture was sparse and old-fashioned, and the carpet threadbare. I got up, looked out of the window at the deserted slope. A slight mist hung over the top of the sycamores and it must have rained in the night because the branches were dripping with raindrops. I began to brush my hair in front of the Victorian wood-framed oval mirror, that swayed back and forth in its cherry-wood stand. The traffic, invisible beyond the trees and the iron gate, was heavy, continuous but muted.

After breakfast in the dining-room the vicar went off to his study and the two maids came in for morning prayers. These, which were once held in the vicar's study, had become less formal since Robert had more or less left home to work in London, and my future mother-in-law held them herself in the dining-room. Her religion was so much part of her that her praying had a spontaneity about it that entirely disarmed criticism, and though I was filled with astonishment by the scene, I immediately felt its comforting warmth, and I suddenly ceased to have any doubts at all about the certainty of my marriage. After we had listened to a few verses from the New Testament and prayed for the King, the Queen and the Prince of Wales, who had just come back from India and was regularly falling off his horse while hunting, my future mother-in-law made a sign to the cook that she could, as usual, remain for a few moments while the menus of the day were gone over. The cook, incidentally, had brought in a copybook, which she handed to Effie, who opened it on her lap and proceeded to write out with her fountain pen in her beautiful hand the menus agreed between them. This ceremony, like morning prayers, surprised but enchanted me. Perhaps I felt that I was experiencing the apprenticeship of a future housewife.

All that day I followed Effie round, when she invited me to do so, otherwise I waited in whatever room we happened to be until she returned. If, as often happened, we were in her Little Room, and she was called out for something, I would look with wonder and fascination at the small, square osier basket which seldom left her side and in which she kept, among other things, her large Bible, her cheque-book on Coutts in the Strand, an embroidered handkerchief, her massive bunch of keys, her fountain pen and the knitting which she took up as soon as she had a moment to herself. Her knitting intrigued me and having asked her permission to do so I timidly took it up, examining the needles which instead of being in steel were in bone, and when I remarked on this she said that steel needles not only tended to give her rheumatism in the fingers but were noisy, whereas bone needles were neither noisy nor did they appear to have any harmful effect on her almost chronic rheumatism. Effie's basket won me over completely. It was full of such essentially feminine treasures. Her facility in writing cheques and letters astonished me. She had an immense mail and when answering it she would sit down on the sofa or the nearest chair and, placing a pad on her lap, allow her fountain pen to run across the paper with a facility of thought and action never disturbed by my presence beside her. Her small, clear, exquisite hand doubtless came in part from the fact that she wrote as she talked or breathed, almost continually when she was not knitting, and in part from her mother, Peli, whose writing I was later to discover was in every way similar. So, for that matter was her sister's. For Effie had a sister called Helen who at one time had acted as a sort of social secretary to their mother when Peli lived at Hans Place, Knightsbridge, and who later went to China as a missionary. As for Effie's cheques, they seemed to my still girlish eyes to fall from her lovely ringed fingers like the leaves in autumn. It had never struck me that housewives could exist who had no need to ponder over the sums they expended. And not only the sums expended for their household necessities but in a golden shower of charity. For she gave continually, not allowing the right hand to know what the left was doing.

The little maid came into the room and said something. Somebody had called to see her. She was back in a few moments, and taking up her knitting, explained that it was a girl who had found a job in London and was anxious for a reference. 'Though both her father and her brother fought in the trenches during the war,' said Effie, 'she remains for me a little girl.'

'Tell me about the war,' I said. 'While I was a little girl walking beside my father along the banks of the Seine at Clichy, you were all watching those tugs gliding past your garden on the Thames. Was it as bad with you as it was with us?'

'I doubt if it was very different,' said Effie. 'Brentford sent an enormous contingent of men to the front—and they were all my boys. I knew every single one of them. A large number had been in my Bible Class, and I loved them all like sons. The bad news nearly always came to me here as quickly as to the wives, indeed often quicker so that it fell to me to announce it to the womenfolk. For instance, I remember having to go to that girl's family. The girl who is going to take a job in London and who wants a reference. Her mother had given birth to the youngest baby while the father had been on leave a few weeks earlier. He had held it in his arms before going back to the trenches. But he would never see it again. The news came to me first, and I pictured my arrival at the house in Pottery Lane having to tell the wife that her husband had been killed at Mons. I thought she would probably be rocking the baby in her arms as I had seen her so often doing. I was seized with panic at the thought that she might drop it. I knocked timidly at the door and when she opened it, there she was, exactly as I had imagined her, holding the baby in the bend of an arm and smiling with happiness at the sight of me. She said: "How nice of you to come. You're just in time for a cup of tea." And she started asking me a whole lot of questions, which I answered rapidly with a terrible lump in my throat. How long could I put off the fatal moment? Sweetly she smiled down at the baby and then at me, and she wanted me to see how the little thing was trying to put its arms round her neck to embrace her. All the time the word Daddy kept on falling from her lips. "Won't Daddy be proud? Daddy who is so bravely fighting in the trenches."

The sun had come out in all its strength and had turned the river at full tide into ripples of silver and gold. What a magnificent view from the vine-framed windows of the Little Room, and how peaceful the sight of my future mother-in-law with her lovely white hair studded with beautiful tortoise-shell combs. How fresh were her cheeks and how blue were her eyes! I caught myself wondering if she would allow me to love her? She put down her knitting and said:

'Would you like us to pray together? It might help us to think more clearly.' Of course, that was precisely what we needed—to think more clearly. Had I ever asked myself to consider the immensity of the problems I was bringing into her life? Into the lives of everybody in this house? We knelt side by side on the blue Persian carpet. I recall the beauty of its thickness and the intensity of its shades. Side by side—the future mother-in-law and her daughter-in-law. Words fell from her lips without hesitation. She never paused to look for one. She had a wealth of vocabulary that allowed her most secret thoughts to translate themselves into simple, lovely English prose. A clear limpid stream of exquisite English rose heavenwards without a trace of effort on her part to do anything but to commune with a friend. What she was doing was with her perfectly natural. She spoke to God as she spoke to her husband, or to me, or to her little maid. I believe her to have been the nearest approach to a perfect woman I have ever had the privilege to know.

Her Little Room was bathed after this in our common relief and joy. It was a small museum of precious objects—paintings, drawings, German and Italian vases, books, and her large Bible, which is beside me as I write these words nearly half a century later. On every single one of its more than one thousand pages, the wide margins are covered with notes in her exquisite hand—in

English, in Greek, in Latin, in French. Her Greek alphabet is a joy to the eye, as clear and minute as print, and at the end of the Bible, after the coloured maps, pages of her reflections, probably used as a basis for her Bible Classes, and the letters she sent out regularly to lighthouse men all along our British coasts. Robert told me how as a child he would sit at the dining-room table beside her, while she printed off on a little machine her Lighthouse Letters, and then despatched them in parcels with the magazines of those days—*The Strand* magazine, the *Wide World*, and so on. No wonder that she had sons and daughters who wrote to her from all over the world, and whom she considered as her children. On the title page of her Bible, I read in her dear hand:

> When thou readest what here is writt
> Let thy best practice second it;
> So twice each precept read shall be—
> First in ye booke and next in thee.

and under these lines in French, as if something had forewarned her that a stranger from a strange land would one day come to carry away her son:

> O Dieu de vérité, pour qui seul je soupire,
> Unis moi donc à toi par de forts et doux noeuds.
> Je me lasse d'ouir, je me lasse de lire,
>   Mais non pas de te dire:
>   'C'est toi seul que je veux'.   Corneille.

But she was essentially English, albeit proudly in part Scottish through her father, Sir Coutts Lindsay, and had spent much of her childhood at Balcarres in Fife, the favourite boyhood home of Sir Coutts and his younger brother, the future Lord Wantage—'Uncle Bob'. I like this other quotation also written out in her hand:

From every town and village, and little hamlet in England, there is a road to London. So from every text in the Bible there is a road to the Metropolis of Scripture, that is Christ. Whatever text, therefore, you read, say: Now which is the road to Christ?

Followed by:

> Could we with ink the ocean fill,
> And were the skies of parchment made,
> Was every stem on earth a quill,
> And every man a scribe by trade,
> To write the love of God to man
> Would drain the ocean dry,
> Nor could the scroll contain the whole,
> Though stretched from sky to sky.

On this first morning in my future mother-in-law's Little Room, I had the impression that she lived, bathed in her faith, not only in the effervescence of her riverside parish but also amongst her forbears of three or four generations past, so many of whom had helped to make English history. Her humble Bible Class mothers in the Pottery Road or in Green Dragon Lane (I loved the names of the Brentford streets), weighed no less importantly in the scale of her tenderness than these famous names who had peopled her mother's vital, colourful, political and artistic world. But as in the case of her prayers, she was never self-conscious about any of them. Everything and everybody, to her, were as natural as natural could be.

There was a narrow strip of sunflowers embroidered with gold thread on a deep green velvet background, the whole framed in gold. Was Peli also a needlewoman? How comforting to reflect that her learning did not prevent her from being feminine. Here on a low table was a painting of the original Rothschild house in the Judengasse at Frankfurt. As I was looking at it, Effie asked:

'Did you ever read the Hans Andersen tale of the peeping moon?'

'I read it last night in bed.'

She appeared surprised:

'How so?'

'In a slim little volume written by your mother called *Green Leaves*.'

'It is a very pretty story. The house you are looking at is the one into which the moon peered. I gave the volume to Robert but I doubt if he has time to read it.'

'I shall treasure it for both of us,' I said, 'if I may?'

'Then it shall be yours as well as his,' she answered.

'Is it true that the old lady in the story was your great-great grandmother?'

Effie smiled:

'It does sound a long way back,' she said. 'Too far, I fancy, for the imagination of a young girl like yourself.'

'Oh no!' I exclaimed. 'When I was little the people in our street when asked for something they could not afford would say: "Do you take me for a Rothschild!"'

My future mother-in-law laughed.

'How refreshing you are!' she said. 'I'll try to explain. One of the sons whom the Moon saw bowing to the old lady came to England to make his fortune. His four brothers founded branches in various European cities. Because there were five of them, they became the five arrows of the red shield. You will see their hanging sign if ever you walk down St Swithin's Lane in the City. The one who came to England and founded the London house was Mr N. M. de Rothschild. Or Nathan as some people called him. He became the most powerful of the five and the story goes that he was first to obtain news of the result of the Battle of Waterloo by having a message sent to him by a carrier-pigeon. So he was able to buy the Funds when they were depressed.

'He had a daughter called Hannah, a very pretty, intelligent girl but in the beginning a trifle spoilt, I feel sure, because she was given a harp of pure gold, and was taught music by Mendelssohn and Rossini. She had a waist so narrow that a man could span it with his two hands. I also was very proud of my waist when I was a girl. It measured only 21 inches. But of course we wore very tightly laced stays.'

She looked at me wondering if I was bored.

'At the age of nineteen, Hannah was sent on a holiday to her Rothschild cousins in Paris. Nathan's brother, Baron James, had married Betty, daughter of Solomon who had founded the house in Vienna. So you see that the five arrows were already bound very closely together. This was to prove their strength—the policy of what became known as the bundle of sticks. Hannah was received with much affection. Baroness James had arrived as a married

44

woman in Paris when she was scarcely out of the schoolroom, but she quickly used her gifts to start a salon, and she had succeeded in bringing together men who were famous in politics and literature. Hannah's beauty made a great impression on Ary Scheffer, the French painter, who was a constant visitor to the Rothschild house. He began to paint her portrait. It now hangs in the nursery upstairs. I don't know whether you saw it. Remind me to point it out to you next time we go upstairs. The artist never had an opportunity to finish it.'

'How so?'

'Baroness James arranged to give a ball in honour of her young niece, and Hannah was fitted with a dress of white satin, cut narrow in the skirt, with a trimming of small red roses. The sleeves were tight at the elbows, and over this dress she wore a pelerine trimmed with lace. The ball was graced by the King and Queen of the French—Louis Philippe and Marie Amélie. Hannah, in her white satin dress with flowers in her hair, looked like a figure of Dresden china. During the evening she was introduced to Prince Edmond de Clary, wealthy young scion of a noble Viennese family, whose father had travelled to Paris on a mission from the Austrian court at the time of Emperor Napoleon's marriage to Marie-Louise. He no sooner set eyes on Nathan's young daughter than he fell desperately in love with her. They danced together twice, and late in the evening, Prince Clary sought out some person who might be a close friend of Nathan's and willing to go to London to act as his ambassador for Hannah's hand. His choice fell on Prince Esterházy, who knew Nathan intimately and who was generally reputed to be the most extravagant diplomat in Europe, and had scandalized Englishmen by his habit of shaking his Hungarian jacket on the floor of a ballroom for the pleasure of seeing women scramble for the pearls and diamonds that fell from it.

'But Nathan stormed when he heard the news, and immediately sent a courier to Paris to order his daughter's return. She left so hurriedly that Ary Scheffer never had time to finish his portrait.'

My future mother-in-law smiled rather sadly.

'True love in my family has never run smooth,' she said. 'Hannah was to experience another trial, even more turbulent than the first. She fell in love with a young English politician, Henry FitzRoy, brother of Lord Southampton, who was already being singled out for a brilliant career. Brought up as a boy by an austerely Calvanistic mother (the father having died early), Henry FitzRoy took life very seriously. He was a man of ardent feelings and deep convictions but when he came into a room, every woman looked up. He stood well over six feet, with thick black hair, bright blue eyes and a ready smile. He wore curly side-whiskers, was a tower of strength and rode a horse to perfection.

'Though Nathan had died two years earlier during a visit to Frankfurt, both families were violently against the marriage. It was at Gunnersbury Park, half a mile from Brentford where Robert and his sister used to play when they were children (did he tell you?) that Hannah spoke to her mother about FitzRoy. His political future was assured. He had been nominated Deputy Lieutenant for the County of Northamptonshire. Mrs N. M. Rothschild, who managed all the members of her family, even when they were fully grown, violently opposed the idea.'

Effie took me gently by the arm and led me to a small table:

'There she is,' she said, pointing to a superb miniature on ivory. 'This is Mrs N. M. Rothschild as a young woman. Hannah always treasured this painting of her mother, but the girl had a will of her own. She was ready to defy the traditions of her family and to take the consequences.'

Effie went on:

'Lionel, Hannah's elder brother, hoping that Hannah might be made to forget, invited FitzRoy to Piccadilly and suggested he should leave England for six months. If at the end of that time, Hannah was still determined to go through with the marriage, the matter might be reviewed.

FitzRoy crossed Europe in 1838 but on his return their love proved stronger than ever. FitzRoy found himself again involved, however, not only in complications with Mrs N. M. Rothschild and her son Lionel, now the head of the London house, but with his own brother, Lord Southampton, a quarrel so fierce (it was over the details of an allowance) that FitzRoy turned on his heels and left the room, and did not speak to his brother again for fourteen years.

'But nothing broke the lovers' troth. For FitzRoy and Hannah there followed two months of happiness. They drove out in Hyde Park, went to the theatre, supped together. The most surprising thing was that Nathan's widow, who more than any member of the Rothschild family had been violently opposed to the marriage, now showed signs of being won over by the charm and goodness of her prospective son-in-law.

'The wedding took place at St George's, Hanover Square. Henry FitzRoy set off from his flat in South Street with his friend Lord Castlereagh. He must have felt very nervous and disappointed. Lord and Lady Southampton had both refused to come. They would spend the day at their estate at Whittlebury. The Rothschilds also would stay away—all except Hannah's young brother, Nathaniel, who had always stood by her. There would be no bridesmaids—no spring flowers from Gunnersbury on this April day. Mrs N. M. Rothschild hesitated—then suddenly made up her mind. Calling her daughter to her side, she declared her intention of accompanying her in a four-wheeler to the church door!

'So here was Nathan's widow sitting rigid and red-eyed in a corner of a common four-wheeler in order to facilitate my pretty young grandmother's runaway match!

'The carriage clattered across the road and drew up beside the church. When Hannah looked up she saw the tall figure of Henry FitzRoy hurrying towards her. Mrs Rothschild rose slightly from her seat, made a friendly gesture to her future son-in-law, and then kissed her daughter before turning away her head. Soon the sound of the four-wheeler died away, carrying Mrs N. M. Rothschild within it.'

'Did the marriage turn out a very happy one?' I asked.

'Such marriages generally do,' said Effie. 'There was such great love on both sides.'

'And was your mother, Blanche—the one you call Peli—the only child?'

'No, there was a boy, Little Arthur, but he fell from his horse in Upper Grosvenor street and died at the age of sixteen.'

Was this the price that Hannah had been made to pay?

And what would happen to me?

3

THE GONG RANG FOR LUNCH. It was the little maid who rang the brass gong under the stairs next to the drinking-water filter and the long narrow window that looked out on the garden and the river. As soon as the gong had rung, the vicar came out of his study and I followed my mother-in-law out of her Little Room.

The meal was extremely simple. There were only the three of us. Effie, who liked to mark the importance she attached to her husband not only because of his ecclesiastical status but also because he was the man of the house, encouraged him to lead the conversation. Lunch was a time when politics and what was happening in the world were lightly touched upon. The vicar was benignly conservative and spent several evenings every week presiding over the Conservative Club to which Mr Stamp, the turncock at the waterworks, and Mr Thomas, the lodge keeper at the Rothschild estate at Gunnersbury, both his faithful church-wardens, belonged. There was also Mr Jones, the lean, rather cadaverous-looking verger, and several of the men who during the day hammered away at those barges that were tied up for repair at the bottom of the garden, but at the other side of the wall. This narrow arm of the river, incidentally, dried up completely at low tide so that the barges tended to lean over at various acute angles in a gluey expanse of mud that had its own rather appealing smell, and allowed the King's swans to waddle across it on their way to the osier eyot.

The vicar was a Yorkshireman who had once been a curate in the Isle of Man. His dream would have been realized if fortune had allowed him to become a bishop and live in a palace however derelict. Effie, though it would have been counter to her principles to seek advancement, either for herself or for her husband, might nevertheless have gladly made up for the meagreness of a bishop's stipend, as she did for a simple clergyman's. She loved him with all the warmth of her generous heart and would have done anything to make her Burr happy. She often reproached him for never asking for anything. It would never have entered his head to spend a penny on himself, and he took a pride in wearing his black clerical suits until they were practically threadbare. They had the date of their purchase (from a firm near Covent Garden which specialized in such clothes) clearly in the lining, so that he would say: 'This one is twenty years old.'

But though he really would have like to be a bishop, at all events in his imagination, the dream was impossible. He had no university degree. This was something that troubled him, even perhaps shamed him, and though he could say quite truthfully (he would never tell a lie!) that he had studied at Oxford, it was not at the university but at Saint Edward's school. His love for Oxford was touching. He loved its towers and spires, its meadows and college gardens, its quadrangles and common rooms—the pink and white hawthorn that dipped its pungently scented branches into the cool waters of the Cherwell on a spring afternoon. He knew all the coats of arms of the colleges, and on a May morning his thoughts would fly away to the hymns on the top of Magdalen tower. And so was it not natural that what he had been unable to obtain for himself he ardently wanted for his son? Newly married to Effie, happy in the assurance of her love, seated on the lawn of the garden at Brentford between the quince tree and the raspberry canes, he had imagined his infant son a grown man. What would he be doing, this flesh of his flesh? He saw him in a white surplice with the blood-red hood of a Doctor of Divinity preaching from the pulpit at Christ Church or Magdalen. He would be the bishop, the don, the learned divine, the Greek scholar whom the father had failed to be.

He had rather too rapidly anticipated his dream. In sending the boy to Eton he made a good beginning but it had not been without a fight. Though Uncle Bob had gone there (he spent happy years in old Judy Durnford's house), Effie had rather turned away from the pomp and circumstance of Peli's life and might have chosen for her son a more modest place of learning.

But Burr wanted it and that was something that was wholly to his credit. It was the one gift that Robert never ceased to be grateful to his father for. Anxious to hasten the process towards higher learning and the coveted red hood, Burr struck up a friendship with no less exalted an Oxford luminary than Sir Herbert Warren, President of Magdalen College and former vice-chancellor of the University. The two men exchanged examples of donnish wit that was said to explode on occasion in the senior common room. They became so engrossed in this exchange of letters that the vicar of Brentford decided to collect and publish them in a book. Fast and furious what Sir Herbert called 'chesnuts', or good stories, travelled by post between the vicarage and the President's lodge at Magdalen. When those from Oxford arrived, the vicar would take them into his study and chuckle over them, standing, as was his custom in front of his schoolmaster-like desk. In the evening he would try them out on Effie while she sat in her favourite chair, a pad on her lap, in case he wanted to dictate something to her.

While Effie had all the tenderness and sensitivity of her feminine ancestors Burr's mind continually went back to his schooldays, remembering what he was, what he would have liked to be. He said that the last words his father, who was a rector, had said to him were: 'Oh, what a boy you are!' And that was something that made him feel proud. As his book took shape, he asked Sir Herbert to write a foreword, which he did, saying: 'Many time-honoured college stories may be at least half as old as the college they haunt. Every successive Rector, and Provost, Warden or Master, tells again the anecdotes he heard in his youth from his own Head or Dean.'

I recall at this lunch Burr's features momentarily lighting up as I asked him to give an example of the stories Sir Herbert sent him, and he said: 'During a concert in Magdalen College Hall, Oxford, a scout went up to the Master of Ceremonies and asked how he could poke the fire without disturbing the music. "Why, to be sure," was the reply, "between the bars!"' And this one reminded him of another: 'Three young wits, passing along the road to Oxford, met a grave old gentleman, with whom they had a mind to be rudely merry. "Good-morrow, Father Abraham," said one. "Good-morrow, Father Isaac," said the next. "Good-morrow, Father Jacob," cried the last. "I am neither Abraham, Isaac, nor Jacob," replied the old gentleman, "but Saul, the son of Kish, who went out to seek his father's asses, and lo! here I have found them!" '

At first the book was titled 'Attic Salt', which was changed when the publishers reported that far too many people ordered it in the hope that it contained a process for exterminating rats in old attics. Effie persuaded Burr to re-title it 'Good Stories from Oxford and Cambridge'. The unwise anticipation consisted in the dedication to Robert, in which Burr was already discounting the ladder of knowledge that he would be climbing (*Deo volente*) at Magdalen.

This was eventually where things went wrong.

Robert went to Magdalen in the Trinity (summer) term of 1920, having escaped by only a few months the war that had mowed down so many of his near contempories.

Though he himself went there straight from Eton, many undergraduates were much older, having served in the trenches, so that there was probably a more mature element than would otherwise have been the case. Magdalen had the aura of having had the Prince of Wales as an undergraduate there only a very short time earlier, which greatly enhanced Sir Herbert Warren's personal pride. But he welcomed Robert warmly and praised him for a general knowledge paper which he claimed, to Burr's delight, was above the average.

This only made things worse. Trinity term proved one of the hottest on record and Robert did little work. He had a nose for news and would stroll from time to time into the Mitre Hotel where famous people who came to visit Oxford stayed. On arrival they wrote their names in a huge visitors' book that stood for all to consult in the hall. It was thus that he read on a certain day the names of the three latest arrivals—Madame Francis de Croisset, the wife of the famous French playwright, Mlle Marie-Laure Bischoffsheim, her daughter by a former marriage to a South African millionaire, and Princess Galitzine, a ravishing young Russian *émigrée* from the horrors of the revolution who was staying as a guest of the de Croissets at their sumptuous home in Paris.

Mme de Croisset was the daughter of the Comte and Comtesse Adheaume de Chevigné, and she represented all that was most fastidious in a dying French nobility. Girls under her care were not allowed to go about without being chaperoned. Nevertheless she came to Oxford to show her daughter and the slim, lovely princess who had so miraculously escaped from Russia the sights of the university city. Oxford and the plays of Shakespeare are necessary subjects of polite conversation in the baggage of any well-educated foreign girl. So she accepted Robert's invitation to lunch the following day. She probably never bargained for the reception he laid on for them.

Once again the morning was a scorcher and the red and white hawthorn as Burr had known it in his time dipped down into the cool waters of the Cherwell. Magdalen has its own landing pier with the punts and skiffs all ready for any undergraduate to take. Robert chose a punt, filled it with champagne and a superbly cooked lunch from the Junior Common Room and embarked his guests upon it. After all, it was at Burr's expense. One paid for nothing in cash. The bills would go home at the end of term.

For ten days Robert entertained the three women as if he were Nathan in person, or Uncle Bob, who was once able to describe himself as 'probably the biggest landowner in England'. Robert had a thought for the future at the back of his mind. Francis de Croisset, whose plays were being performed in several parts of the world, had entertained President Wilson at his Paris home when he had come over to represent the United States at the Versailles Conference. Mme de Croisset, who descended from the Marquis de Sade, attracted by her money and her wit all the great names of French contemporary art and literature. Her friendship would afford a young man arriving one day in Paris with an inquisitive mind an enviable position.

Mme de Croisset went home positively delighted with her visit to Oxford. The sort of welcome she had received from this handsome young man, an undergraduate at Magdalen, whose quarters in college overlooked the deer park, was of a kind that with her experience of the world she was particularly qualified to appreciate. At her instigation her husband wrote to thank the young man—a most charming letter in that elegant French prose of which he was so famous an exponent, its affectionate simplicity making of it a little masterpiece. A few days later followed inscribed copies of all his books and plays. Later again Marie-Laure sent over the newest works of Marcel Proust, Anatole France and others. Doors were already opening.

The success of this enterprise worked insidiously against Burr's dream of an ecclesiastical and scholastic future for his son. It was as if the demon of Peli's interest in the world of art and letters were driving a needle into the young man's veins. Away with bishops and dons and even with Sir Herbert's guiding hand. Robert took an important lead in founding the *Cherwell* magazine and reserved for himself the post of dramatic critic which meant frequent, far too frequent, visits to London—and the heady discovery of the pass door into the prompt corner of many a London stage. To the orchestra pits also, where Arthur Bliss conducting was surrounded by Oxford friends. Thus the life on which Effie as a young woman (having refused the hand of a wealthy nobleman) had resolutely turned her back, and for which Burr had an instinctive dislike, was beckoning the young man away from the paths of duty.

The summer vacation hid the seriousness of what was taking place.

Burr must still have believed that nothing serious had happened to jeopardize the fulfilment of his dreams. He disliked all foreign countries except Switzerland, whose clear air, mountain passes and snow-capped peaks held the same sort of place in his heart as the towers and spires of Oxford. Effie had given him a series of coloured plates depicting the wild flowers that grew on the slopes of the Matterhorn when spring began to melt winter snows. And, of course, there were the gentian and the edelweiss. These pictures hung on the walls of his study together with photographs of certain learned divines. He gave his son a return ticket (third class) by boat and rail for Zermatt, and sent him off with enough cash for a week at an inn. Robert crossed the Channel on a paddle-steamer by the Newhaven–Dieppe night service, arriving at Dieppe at 2 a.m. This was not the first time my fiancé had been to France though it was the first time he had gone alone. Curiously enough Burr, who disliked the French, had evoked his son's interest in the country during the summer of 1912 when he and Effie, who normally took their family for a six weeks' holiday at Rottingdean, decided instead to spend August and the first two weeks in September at Folkestone, where a clergyman put his vicarage at their disposal on condition that Burr took the Sunday services. The tall, narrow house stood on a height that allowed it to dominate the town and the harbour. The view was quite exceptional and it was said that on a clear day one could faintly distinguish the line of the French coast. Burr, who was a splendid swimmer, remaining in the sea for hours at a time when they went to Rottingdean, was an equally determined walker. He took the children along the warren between Folkestone and Dover, where the wild thyme and the blackberries grew just under the railway line. From the windows of their eyrie vicarage house they could see the Folkestone packet leaving at the appointed hour for France. Conversely they could watch the incoming ship from Boulogne. Burr's dislike of the French was mitigated by his love for the sea. Yes, he was English in all his tastes, and what true Englishman does not inherit from his forbears a love for the sea? Burr liked to cross the Channel on the morning packet on the condition that having safely arrived on the other side he could come straight back to England. Once or twice he took Effie but the sea was rough and Effie was terribly sick, and all her love for Burr could not overcome her mistrust of the sea. So Burr took his son and sometimes his daughter Katherine and as they had to waste an hour or two in Boulogne before returning on the next ship, Burr bought them in the colourful market the prettiest French dolls dressed as fisherwomen, and took them to a pastrycook's shop where they each ate a *baba au rhum*, a concoction so strange and delightful to the two English children that it made the journey memorable.

Yes, fate did indeed cause Burr to work against himself. All the more so because it was during this summer holiday in Folkestone that Peli in London became suddenly ill and died. Effie, who hitherto had never left her family for a single night, rushed to London, leaving the children in the care of Burr who, left to himself, and to take his mind off his wife's troubles, repeated those exciting trips across the Channel.

But for Robert on his way to Switzerland there was a whole new world to explore. It seems incredible that there were still a few paddle-steamers left on the night service of the Newhaven–Dieppe route but when the sea was calm, and the moon shone in a clear, warm sky, it was wonderful to be standing on the deck waiting to set foot on a foreign soil. After the ship had docked, the scene at the marine station at 2 a.m. was one of immense activity and colour. The war had not been over for so very long and the cross-channel services were packed with people of every kind now going about their business or their pleasure after so many years of being confined in their own lands. There were military commissions, diplomats, politicians, engineers planning rebuilding on scarred battlefields, and an immense number of American trippers who swarmed over Europe with their bags and trunks covered with stick-on labels from the famous hotels of the Continent. They were wealthy, heady with the experience of having made the Atlantic crossing on a famous liner and determined to soak up this rich, colourful atmosphere of post-war Europe in the throes of tumultuous rebirth. As the long queues formed to pass through passport control and customs, Robert looked on the busy restaurant from which emanated the most appetizing odours of French cuisine, on the long trains drawn up behind their powerful Pacific locomotives, these ready to set forth for all those romantic cities which from childhood had filled his imagination: the Simplon-Orient express with the names of Venice, Zagreb and Athens on the blue sleeping-cars; the Nord Express for Brussels and Amsterdam; the longest train of all for Paris—Saint Lazare—with its first- and second-class couchettes, its heated compartments from which issued jets of boiling, hissing steam.

Along the platform between the drawn-up trains, women wearing *képis* and black overalls wheeled trolleys, some of which contained sandwiches, cakes and bottles of brandy; others newspapers and magazines; others pillowcases and blankets for hire. With what skill did these women manoeuvre their wares between the crowd of passengers who had already passed the customs and the blue-bloused porters with their wide, red cotton belts preceding them with the heavy luggage, and expertly looking out for a suitable couchette or a spare corner seat.

Beyond all this the town slept. A porter told Robert that the Paris train would not leave for at least forty minutes. Yes, he could go and explore. There were no barriers. He could come and go as he pleased especially if he had no luggage. So he made his way out to the fish-market, crossed the rails into the little main street with its picturesque arcades, was charmed by the quaintness of the little shops and, hearing distantly the sound of the sea against shingles, turned into a narrow, medieval street where a man naked to the waist and wearing a paper cap was thrusting dough into his fiery wood-heated oven. The smell of freshly baked bread mingled with the smell of the sea breaking against the shingles at 2 a.m. was irresistible. The man turned round, saw the stranger and said: 'If you would fancy a hot roll, take one from the tray behind you but don't burn your tongue!' As he ate it, amused to find himself, except for the baker, the only wakeful person in the middle of this sleeping seaside French town, Robert's mind went back to an afternoon at Brentford when he had sat with Effie in her Little Room. Effie was holding some faded letters written by her mother, Peli, at the age of eleven, to her father, the young politician whom Hannah had married in such lonely circumstances. Blanche and her brother Arthur, the little boy who had injured his spine when thrown from a horse in a London street, had been taken by Hannah to Dieppe. He had passed their hotel. He remembered the name—the Royal Hotel, a very modest, slate-faced building. As these documents eventually all came into my possession, I can transpose their contents back across time. I know what I did not know when that day at Brentford I sat between Effie and Burr at lunch, wondering what to say. But to understand what was going on in their minds not only about me but about their feelings towards their son, I must eliminate the element of time.

Hannah with her two children, Blanche and Arthur, in the month of July 1855, crossed to Boulogne for the sake of the shorter sea voyage, but as there was no railway between Boulogne and Dieppe, they went by train to Abbeville, travelling in their own barouche, which was fastened on a truck at the end of the train. Both children wrote letters to their father, describing this journey, at the end of which they were bruised all over. For nearly eight hours they sat in the barouche with their backs to the engine watching the ground slip from under their feet with what appeared to them appalling velocity. After staying for a while at the Royal Hotel, Hannah found a comfortable apartment on the first floor of a house overlooking the front. There was a broad balcony with an awning, and a garden where Arthur would lie for long hours watching the ships through his telescope. Blanche found that a number of children occupied the floor above them, but most of all she longed for her best playfellow, her father. She and Arthur wrote letters a few days after their arrival.

July 9 1855

My dear Pa,

We have removed from the Royal Hotel and are now at Madame Hallouin's pleasant little house where we occupy the rooms on the first floor. In the same house above us is a little boy, a little Count de Montebello. He has a large india-rubber ball, a kind of balloon, and he and I and another little girl who lives here also, play together. Sometimes I stand on our balcony whilst they are in the garden and then we throw the ball to each other in turns. By the by it would be just the thing for you and me, would it not? There is a little fountain in the garden here which is now playing. I like Dieppe very much and I think you would like to sit out on our wide balcony under the awning. Do all my geraniums thrive with the care I am sure you bestow on them? Do you draw anything now when you cry: "Order! Order!" in the chair, the uncomfortable chair of the House of Commons?"

Good-bye, my dear, dear Pa,
From your affectionate and ever loving daughter,
Blanche.

From what Blanche later told her daughter Effie Dieppe was a pleasant place for them. The picturesque harbour, the bare-legged, costumed fishwives, the shops with their manufactures of delicately worked ivory, the market-place full of fruit and flowers, the old cathedral and the ruined castle on a green hill overlooking the sea were all things to strike them.

But there was one sight that greatly interested Blanche. This was a certain flagstaff which could be seen from Madame Hallouin's balcony, denoting from an early hour every morning whether bathing was practicable or no. If the flag was hanging limply round its mast or floating proudly in the breeze, well and good—Blanche might be sure of bathing. Then the sea was, as old Léon, the bather, expressed it: 'Convenable.' But if the flag was not visible there was no use trying to melt the hearts of the stern bathing men. The bathing huts were locked and Blanche might go home.

She loved bathing; arrayed in a blue-and-red costume, with straw slippers and a hideous oilskin cap, she sallied forth into the ocean hand in hand with her dear Léon who, like all the other bathing men, was a weather-beaten, elderly fisherman, who went out fishing at all times of the year except in summer, when he dipped the ladies and children and taught them to swim. Blanche was not dipped, neither did she receive pails of water on her back or over her head. She used to run knee-deep into the sea and lie down under the first curling wave. The bathing men were jealous of each other, and proud of their pupils.

Old Léon was a good, stern master. He used to hold Blanche by a leather belt that she wore round her waist while she learnt the movements of swimming. Every now and then he would treacherously let her go and when she came up again to the surface, panting and spluttering, he would nod his head and ask ironically: 'Ç'a du sel, hein?' But as time went on Blanche swam away from him into the deep water where another old fisherman called Pierre, and not unlike Charon, used to navigate in a small open boat, on one side of which was a short ladder whereon tired swimmers used to perch and rest, and from the upper step of which they took delightful headers into the sea.

An enjoyable epilogue to these bathes was the hot fresh-water footbath in the hut. Blanche would then go to a booth close to the beach where an old woman in a large, clean white apron sold hot cakes powdered with sugar. And so home to breakfast. Once she went for a donkey ride and even took part in a donkey race to amuse her brother. She and her governess each rode a donkey. Another of these animals was harnessed to Arthur's bath-chair and his tutor, Mr Sims, bestrode a fourth. Mr Sims was tall and his legs so long that he could almost walk while riding the donkey, so it ended by his getting off and dragging the animal after him. Blanche had taken a fancy to a white donkey which she begged to be allowed to mount. She patted it affectionately, and inquired its name.

'Mademoiselle Blanche,' was the answer.

In the market-place they bought fresh flowers and ripe peaches, but the day they looked forward to was that on which the *place* was given up to the sale of trousers. There was always a strong smell of cloth and wool about the neighbourhood. Coats, waistcoats and other articles of attire were hung out to view, while a sturdy female standing in an open cart sold garments by auction and harangued the multitude:

'Tenez, Messieurs, Mesdames,' she would vociferate: 'voici votre affaire. Un petit pantalon tout ce qui a de plus fin. Magnifique. Mirobolant. Un vrai pantalon d'Empereur!'

If her sales were not as successful as she desired, this energetic lady apostrophized some unfortunate, shy youth in the crowd, remarking on the shabby state of his lower garment, causing much derisive laughter and many jokes which warmed and cheered the country folk.

Once every week also there was the travelling dentist. A loud booming drum announced his arrival, and an enormous pink umbrella overhung a species of scaffold, from which he addressed the people beneath. The drum lapsed into silence during the persuasive speech of the dentist, at the close of which there was always some unfortunate brought forward by friends who comforted him and patted him on the back, but were none the less ready to be amused at his expense. The wretch was in most cases a big hulking, good-natured fellow in a blue-checked blouse, whose very swelled face was tied in a pocket handkerchief. Amidst the applause of the populace he mounted the steps of the scaffold and the spider, having once secured his prey, pinned him down in a large armchair, and half covered his face with an enormous crimson pocket handkerchief, which was probably to conceal the blood of his victim. He then extracted the tooth whilst the drum, at its very loudest, covered up all cries and expostulations. With a low bow, the dentist showed the tooth to the multitude, daintily holding it in his forceps. There was a murmur of admiration, whilst another victim was hustled to the front and even sometimes sarcastically urged on by his predecessor. It was at the corner of this market-place that Hannah heard of the taking of Sevastopol in the Crimea. She and her children were standing outside the pastrycook's when an old veteran with glittering eyes told them the news. The whole town was in a state of great delight. The French and English were by way of being great friends and even the market women spoke with tears of the dear English soldiers. Blanche and Arthur invested in a couple of coloured candles, which they stuck outside their window to aid the general illumination that took place at night-fall.

Meanwhile Captain Robert Lindsay, whose elder brother, Sir Coutts, Blanche would eventually marry (but this was far from the thoughts of the little girl of eleven) was writing home from the Guards' Camp, 11th September 1855:

'Sebastopol is at last in the hands of the allies. For eleven months have we been within a mile of a town which we dared hardly look at, much less approach, and now it is ours to do what we like with, at least, so much of it as remains, for the fire has been raging three days and is still burning. . . . The Russians left the town on fire in fifty places, all the public buildings and barracks ruined, and with trains laid. After their departure the most tremendous explosions took place in all directions, barracks, museums, churches all going up into the air like fireworks. At 5 a.m. we sent a party down to the Redan to bury the dead, who were lying there in hundreds. I rode through . . . the panic in the main street became general, and the rush of the crowd tremendous, drunken soldiers and sailors, French and English, tumbling over one another, and those on horseback, riding over them.'

The locomotive of the Paris train gave an enormous shriek that echoed over the sleeping town. Robert, the Robert who bore Captain Lindsay's Christian name, ran to the quays, where he leapt onto the train as it was beginning slowly to move along the rails that went through the town. The huge locomotive trembled and shook, for the rails were laid on a surface of street cobble-stones. And so to the town station, where it paused for a few moments.

Then starting off again it gathered speed and rushed through the night. 'Don't look out of the window,' his father, the vicar, had said, 'there's nothing worth seeing as you cross France.' But half an hour later when the train stopped at Rouen—Rive Droite, Robert jumped out on the platform and walked briskly into the station yard. He wanted to visit this city where Joan of Arc had been burnt at the stake. The station clock said 4 a.m.'

4

As soon as lunch was over, Burr went back to his study, Effie and I to her Little Room. She sat down and opened her large Bible, telling me that she had a Bible Class to prepare. It was the afternoon for her Mothers' Meeting, which took place in what was known as the Green School, adjoining the church.

'May I come with you?' I asked.

'Are you sure, child?' she asked. But she could see from my earnest expression that her query was unnecessary. She appeared to forget my presence from then onwards, engrossed in what she was reading, and I interpreted this as yet another sign that she had already accepted me into the family. My eyes fell on a small oval painting of a delicate, fair-haired boy of ten or eleven reclining on a hard couch, his head reposing on a lace-trimmed white pillow, and his left hand, as white and slender as a girl's, stretched out in front of him. On a low table by the couch was an open book.

'Was this Little Arthur?' I asked.

My mother-in-law looked up from her Bible, followed my gaze and said:

'Yes.'

She seemed to consider the matter a moment and went on:

'Why don't you run up and get your copy of Peli's *Green Leaves*. You could read what she says about him while I prepare my little talk to the mothers.'

So I went to fetch the book in which Peli had written:

'I have in mind the story of two short lives. One is that of a lifeboat, for the building of which my mother left a sum of one thousand pounds as a gift in memory of her only son, my brother; the other life is that of my brother himself. The lifeboat, named the *Arthur Frederick*, was stationed at Rye, and, as I believe, rescued many people from a watery grave; after sixteen short years it was worn out, and the work of it was over. The human life of Arthur Frederick FitzRoy lasted sixteen years all but one month, and then flickered out, having always been deprived of much longed-for activity, but leaving to a small home-circle an abiding example of courageous patience and silent endurance.

'He was, in early childhood, a splendid boy. During his second year, spent at Naples with his parents, the nurse was frequently accosted in daily walks by strangers asking: "Who is that magnificent boy?" and for several years he continued in magnificent health and beauty. He was taught to ride early and fearlessly, as are most of the FitzRoys; but, alas, one day when he was scarcely six years old, he was riding down our street—Upper Grosvenor Street—when something caused the pony to shy and throw him on a heap of flints prepared for mending the road, and thus his spine was irretrievably injured. I—two years younger—can just remember his being carried into the house—the bustle and excitement.

'For some months the surgeons did not know how, or to what extent, he was hurt; he was ordered gymnastics and active exercise. Only after a time was it found necessary to keep him absolutely quiescent, lying on a couch where, but for one short break of a different treatment when he was about eight or nine, he lay for ten years, growing weaker, paler, thinner, till, a month before his sixteenth birthday, he passed away.

'My mother, Hannah, devoted herself to him all she could, though endeavouring to advance my father's political career as much as in her lay. We all often went abroad in search of doctors, and my mother denied herself nearly every society pleasure in order to stay at home with her boy, cheering him, talking to him, making poultices, and so on.

'For, as years went on, his life became more filled with pain. At one time he was condemned to lie at full length on a board that was covered only with scanty red cloth, and where there was a hole for his head to sink into. Once he fell off the board and hurt his knees. This brought additional torture; leeches, among other remedies, were applied. I remember one afternoon that we spent together, when a leech dropped and I had to pick it up and place it on his knee again. And, oh! how well I remember the horrid sight of leeches in a plateful of salt, disgorging.

'Arthur must have had great endurance, even as quite a little boy, for I cannot call to mind any impatient or discontented word. Learning stole quietly into his life and into his heart. The Latin and Greek languages became to him as easy as his own English tongue, especially when, after some years of suffering, he was allowed an easier couch, on which, at his elbow, a couple of stout and erudite tomes usually lay.

'One of his earliest joys was the reading of Cornelius Nepos. He was then eight, I was six, and fired by his enthusiasm, I, too, loved to dream of Egeria in her laurel grove, and to recite a few of Macaulay's stirring Lays.

'But he soon passed beyond my childish sympathy in study, and when presently it came to the reading of Thucydides, I was left far behind. Then, indeed, he spent a great part of his days with a tutor, and I with my governess, the more so as I never had any sisters, and worked hard in girlish lines apart from him.

'Nevertheless, there were many pleasant holiday times for us— times when we went up and down the sea-front, he in his long, spinal chair, I walking beside him, consulting mysteriously what we should do were the French to invade England, for this was before the day of the Entente Cordiale. I believe the part assigned to me in such a contingency was to stand on the roof of the house and throw large rocks down on the heads of the storming intruders. It was a matter of quite secondary importance that rocks might not be at hand, to say nothing of the difficulty of lifting and throwing them.

'Another favourite pastime was to clear the large table in Arthur's schoolroom and conduct a toy fight upon it with tin soldiers and diminutive cannon. I described this some years ago in a book called *A String of Beads* and I will insert part of the little poem here:

> 'Tis raining—we're unable
>   To take our walk to-day:
> Let's clear the schoolroom table,
>   And have a battle play.

Arthur's the red-coat leader,
  Blanche takes the French 'mossoos':
She pouts, but none will heed her—
  She's much too young to choose.

Tin are the warriors eager,
  They stand where'er you please;
Our wooden guns are meagre
  But loaded full with peas.

The French marshal sues for quarter,
  And mourns her weak campaign;
Smiles—she's but half a tartar—
  May the English win again!

'But as my brother grew older, our schoolrooms being separate, he amused himself often by bird-stuffing and arranging a collection of eggs; moreover, he became an expert shot at a pistol range, though books and study remained his chief delight. His fifteenth birthday was a grief to him. He had never quite given up the hope of a midshipman's life. He loved the sea and all regarding it, and every old sailor at Brighton, Dover, or Folkestone, knew and welcomed the boy with the beautiful serious face who lay so patiently in his spinal chair, and gazed lovingly out through his little telescope at every passing ship.

'Perhaps I saw more of him than usual the few months before he died. We were then living at Paris. I remember the evening drives we were allowed to take in a barouche (that had been brought over for his benefit, and which was long enough to admit his couch), and the great ideas, great plans that we conjured up for the future. He was to travel, to learn Arabic. He never willingly relinquished his hold on life, nor his hopefulness.

'His death was sudden and painless. My mother was standing by the window of his bedroom. The maid had just brought in his breakfast on a tray; he put down with a little sigh the big Greek dictionary that was on his bed, and forthwith passed gently out of this world of pain, where he had borne himself bravely and uncomplainingly as a man—perhaps he himself would have liked to say as an Englishman. His nature was affectionate, but it was to my mother, Hannah, that he gave the great measure of love that must have sustained him in manifold sufferings.

'Our parents were both of them broken-hearted. I do not think that my father ever recovered from the grief of his only son's death; he himself died in the following year. My mother's pain was intense.

'And I—it seems to me but yesterday that my brother died; the whole house had revolved around his narrow couch. The evening before his death he sent for me. He had put on for warmth a little scarlet comforter and muffetees that I had knitted for him. He was not demonstrative; he rarely put his affection into words; he hated kissing, and, still more, any expressions of sympathy. But that evening, when I entered his room, he said: "Kiss me, Blanchy," and we wound our arms about each other, as though we had been little children again, though I did not guess that this was to be our last good-bye.

'Four or five years ago, when I was at Paris, I went to see the house in the Avenue Gabriel where we had lived. It seemed to be shut up and deserted. The day was gloomy, and the trees opposite the house were leafless and gloomy also. On the window-sill of the room that had been my brother's sat a solitary dove.

After his death the following poem was found among his papers, dated a few weeks earlier:

> Hail Silence! Queen of Night and soft Repose,
> Thou welcome refuge of a troubled breast,
> Thou grateful solace of unuttered woes,
> Thou best of friends, giver of peace and rest.

I was about to close the book when I saw another mention of Little Arthur's death in a subsequent pamphlet. Blanche was talking about dreams, and she wrote:

'It is a paradox but true, that some of our pleasantest dreams bring us the most sorrow. When some loved one is dead, he or she often seems to return to us in sleep, and the old and happy days have come again. But ah! the awakening, the heart-break! On the other hand, I wonder whether many people dream painfully, as I have sometimes done, of the plaint of a dear one.'

Blanche here breaks into verse again:

There is a dream—I have dreamt it oft—I dream it now and
    again,
While the sensitive strings of my soul vibrate till they murmur
    and cry for pain,
Before me he lies, the brother I loved—his fair and open brow
By suffering touched, a flower in frost; 'twas wont to be so,
    'tis now;
'How long?' he asks, and his pale hand droops from the big
    Greek tome at his side,
'How long have you left me here forgot, unloved, untended,
    denied?'

The oval miniature of the boy painted on ivory stood on its gilt
frame. Like so many of the treasures in Effie's Little Room it was
to pass into my possession even before her death. Unworthy
custodians of these sacred memories, we took too many of them,
including Little Arthur's miniature, to our farm in France, where
they were pillaged by the village population during the advance
of the victorious German Army in 1940, and doubtless sold by
guilty men to art dealers at Caen, where they would have been
destroyed during the aerial bombardments which preceded the
Anglo-American storming of the beaches four years later. How
right, he was, Effie's Burr, to fear the alien influence which he saw
stealthily entering into his house like a thief in the night.

My mother-in-law went up to her bedroom to put on a hat—
and I followed her, anxious to participate in what must have been
small rituals infinitely repeated. At the top of the stairs we
turned right, passing through the room that had formerly been
Robert's but which Burr now used for his morning ablutions.
Here, facing the windows which looked out on his beloved garden
and the river, he would shave with one of those old-fashioned
cut-throat razors which he clung to as if out of respect for his
youth. Effie also used this room, so light and airy, as a linen room,
most of Peli's sheets and pillow-cases from Hans Place having
been brought here in 1912. Lavender bags from the garden
reposed between the linen sheets, Effie having always liked to

make lavender bags every summer as she also made quince and apple jam. The quince tree opposite the windows of Effie's Little Room had fruit that hung from its low boughs like pure gold, looking just like the trees in magic gardens portrayed in the coloured plates in those fairy-tale books which Mr Leopold de Rothschild (Uncle Leo) gave Robert for Christmas.

When Uncle Leo who was King Edward VII's friend, happened to be at Gunnersbury Park, an estate which had been in the family since Napoleonic times, he would send for the children, if they happened to be with their German nurse in the park, so that he could cut them a slice from one of those famous chocolate cakes sent to him from Vienna. Peaches and grapes grew in his heated glass-houses, birds from tropical lands flew in the aviary and the flower beds in front of the house were in high summer full of heliotrope, or cherry-pie as the gardeners called it, whose sweet smell perfumed the air. With the approach of autumn, Uncle Leo would ask: 'And what would you like for Christmas?' He expected no immediate answer. The matter was too weighty, and so in due course a letter would have to be written under the guidance of Mallalal in the schoolroom. It was a modest request for a book of fairy-tales that brought all the many volumes edited by Andrew Lang, each being bound in a different colour so that it bore the name of its particular hue—The Blue Fairy Book, The Red Fairy Book, and so on. Robert, who once inexplicably asked for an exotic plant to put on the schoolroom table, received a model hothouse 4 feet long and as many high, made like a real one minutely to scale, with hot pipes and a glass roof, and filled with miniature Japanese and Mexican trees and plants and cacti, so that a place had to be found for it by the window under the stairs between the luncheon gong and the machine for making filtered water. In the stables beside the house at Gunnersbury, Uncle Leo kept the curricles, coaches, barouches, four-in-hands, etc that the Rothschilds had used not only for travelling between Gunnersbury, then in the heart of the country, and their office in New Court in St Swithin's Lane in the City, but also for journeys across Europe, such as to Frankfurt. All this, I fancy, was to have its influence on Robert's impressionable mind. Though never showing much interest in money, he was to live in a perpetual fairy-tale, full of wonder and surprise at the world about him, inquisitive, with an instinctive nose for news, but averse to any work of a concentrated kind.

But I left Effie putting on a hat in the bedroom with the immense double bed. Burr took a cold bath every morning in the antiquated bathroom overlooking the slope. It would not have been much good trying to have a hot one because the water in the hot tap merely gurgled and died, the boiler dating from the Victorian era and long past its useful life. Effie took a bath in the bedroom, a hot one, in a hip bath with a huge back to it like those wicker chairs one used to see at the seaside. The little maid would bring her up cans of hot and cold water and, modestly screened from view, she would sponge herself with beautiful, expensive sponges bought at dear Harrods.

Well, here she was with a hat, very difficult to describe, hiding her lovely white hair, and giving her the appearance of a famous actress in disguise. Now she had everything, her Bible, her keys, and the notes she had prepared for her talk to the mothers, the grandmothers, the mothers-in-law! I followed her downstairs, waited while she peeped into her Little Room to be sure she had forgotten nothing and then we crossed the hall and were soon on the slope.

The High Street smelt first of gas and then of beer, or conversely according to the direction of the wind. Incredible though it seems, this part of it was as far as Effie and the vicar were concerned not very different from a village. The restless, noisy, clanging traffic was, of course, for the most part without human soul or feature, and who could tell, except for the tram drivers, whence they had come and to what rendezvous they were going? But everybody else, every shopkeeper looking out of his door, and almost every single person walking along the pavement, was potentially a member of Effie's immense family who had probably been christened by the vicar, married by him, helped at one time or another, spiritually or financially, by Effie. As she was very deaf and not very quick in reaction, for the most part absorbed in her thoughts and dreams, she was never quite sure if she were being greeted or not, or whether it behoved her to stop and inquire of this or that person who *looked* as if he wished to speak to her, what the matter could be. To walk in the street with my future mother-in-law was therefore a nerve-racking, jerky business, but coal men seated on their wooden bench, their sacks on their heads arranged like coal-black sails, their features grimy, their boots immense and hobnailed, greeted us in a manner that left me in no doubt about their affection for her. Her kingdom may have been one of evil smells and smoking stacks, but it had a homely similarity to the factory-ridden Clichy of my youth, which endeared it to me. How could Robert possibly have imagined that he need be ashamed of his riverside birthplace?

I am not quite sure why this adjunct to the church should have been called the Green School. I have an idea that my mother-in-law once told me but I forget. It was an ugly, cold, tinny building with a sort of stage at one end and a harmonium, and it was on this occasion about half filled with a collection of the most uncouthly dressed women, who would positively have frightened me if I had not noticed the friendly smiles on all their tired, wrinkled faces. Their clothes smelt of damp, dyed wool, and their poor hands were hard and lined with work, and their hats were even more extraordinary than the candle extinguisher that Effie was wearing. Nobody passing the open door would have turned to give our wretched looking assembly a second look, and yet—I have never seen such expressions of affection on a sea of uplifted human faces. Love triumphed over their appalling lack of beauty.

We prayed, we listened to Effie's short address, extempore, without a look at her notes, inspired, as if she had profited by the gift of tongues, and had been given the promise that she would never have to seek the looked-for word but that her prose would come out of her as from a chosen vessel. She paused, went over to the harmonium, announced a hymn and started to play the tune. She played several bars but nobody sang. She looked up puzzled, with that expression of bewilderment that I had noticed in the street when she was not certain whether she should greet a passing parishioner or not. Then from one of the mothers in the hall:

'No, dearie, it's not that one. It's this one.'

'Oh!' said Effie, contrite. 'I'm playing the wrong tune!'

70

'That's right, dear. No. 255. "Just as I am without one plea." '

Without any further show of embarrassment, Effie turned the page and played the correct tune, and all the women sang together:

> Just as I am without one plea
>   But that Thy blood was shed for me,
> And that Thou bidd'st me come to Thee,
>   O Lamb of God, I come.

Mrs Stamp, the wife of the turncock at the waterworks who was the vicar's churchwarden, helped serve the tea. I was introduced all round, and they all called me: 'My dear!' I began to cry. I cry easily but my heart was overflowing. I had seldom felt so immensely happy. On our way back, though one did not joke with Effie, I recalled how affectionately one of the women had put her right about the hymn. She answered very simply:

'Yes, it's a very beautiful hymn. It was my mother's favourite but she never allowed us to sing it in her presence. Her father, my grandfather, Henry FitzRoy, recited the words on his deathbed.'

On my way back to Stacey Street that evening, I was as apprehensive of having to face Matilda as I had been, only twenty-four hours earlier, of facing my future mother-in-law. What would I tell her? Were I to show myself too full of admiration for Effie, I would certainly incite my own mother's possessive jealousy. How could I suggest that it might be possible to love both a mother and a mother-in-law? On reflection, I wonder if while travelling to Hammersmith on top of the tram I was not for the first time preparing to hide the true state of my mind from Matilda, which would inevitably lead to a division of loyalties.

For, in truth, there were certain things that I could not say. That we had suddenly prayed together in the middle of her Little Room—that room in which she was surrounded by the precious heirlooms of her illustrious families, from which beyond the vine-framed windows one could look out on a garden full of flowers and fruit, the silvery waters of the Thames and beyond the towing-path, the tall trees of Kew Gardens. How could one tell that to Matilda who had never enjoyed a moment free from disappointment or fear, fear for the future, fear of illness or of finding herself alone? If out of hurt pride she were to laugh at me, then I would be hurt to the quick.

Love had suddenly come between us—and for Matilda, this thieving love was almost as cruel as death. It was the forerunner of separation. She and I were doomed to part, and that was something that neither of us could do anything about, but which robbed me of much of my joy. Her secret dreams had been so very different. She would have liked me to become a film star, preferably in Hollywood. She knew that I had been approached by several wealthy American directors whose hands I had manicured at the Savoy. She supposed that if they were to take me to Hollywood she would be invited to accompany me. We would have had a fine house with a swimming-pool and she, as my mother, would have blossomed out into my guardian angel. There would have been, at least for a time, no interfering husband to come between mother and daughter. She would have kept me all to herself. And, oh, marvel of marvels, we would have had lots of money in the bank.

Caught up between the Rabelaisian atmosphere of Stacey Street and the sombre if rather monotonous dignity of life at Brentford, I welcomed Robert's return from Geneva. Apart from the problems of our engagement, I was depressed by the precarious state of my health, and the secret knowledge that I would not be able to go on working very long. I needed rest and plenty of fresh air.

Robert, as I have already said, was at that time on the *Morning Post*, a dignified but from his point of view, dull newspaper which, if it gave him leisure to take me out every evening for long suppers at the Ivy or the Carlton Grill, during which moments we were divinely happy, offered little hope of an exciting career. In spite of all these wealthy and famous forbears on the maternal side, he had no fortune of his own except for a very small sum which his mother had given him when he was twenty-one, and which we were spending joyously to augment his salary of nine guineas a week, which even then was not a lot of money.

There was a saying in certain countries that journalism led to everything on the condition of getting out of it. Though this dictum applied less to England than to America, it is nevertheless true that youth is almost the best baggage for the boy or girl who wants to succeed as a reporter. And Robert had gone into it as others became buccaneers several centuries earlier. After helping to found that Oxford magazine during his first summer at Magdalen, he began spending almost more time in London than at Oxford. He had produced a play at Eton. Henry Ainley, during this winter of 1920, invited him to come behind the scenes of the St James's Theatre as often as he liked during the unforgettable run of *Peter Pan*, in which he was playing with Edna Best. Henry Ainley who had been the most beautiful Romeo of his generation, was not only a woman's dream but one of the greatest actors of the period, not as tall and slender as he was before the war, but now solid-looking, with a magnificent voice and unruly black hair. To give a young man like Robert the run of the most romantic of London's West End theatres was a present not to be despised. Between performances Gerald du Maurier would come over from the New Theatre, and because of J. M. Barrie's wards, was always glad to see a former Eton boy. And of course he was also introduced to men like Nigel Playfair and Leon Quartermaine.

By the early spring of 1921, at the end of the Hilary term, Robert, faced with an unprepared Divinity Paper, walked out of the examination room and never returned to Oxford. He knew exactly what he wanted to do and lost no time in doing it. Journalism in those days led to all the vital happenings of the world, with an opportunity to reflect and to write.

Robert's decision to leave Magdalen without a word of explanation to Sir Herbert Warren was less than considerate. His father was twice broken-hearted—by his son's rudeness to a man of such eminence whose friendship Burr valued above any other, and by the fact that his own dream, the dream of a lifetime, of one day seeing his son a don at Oxford in Holy Orders, was shattered. One can imagine how Burr must have felt when he was obliged to write a letter to the President of Magdalen College—the man who had helped him to collect all those wonderful 'chestnuts' about Oxford, who had done him the honour of writing a lengthy introduction to the book, who had so affectionately welcomed Robert into his college—the college that not only had medieval grandeur but the added glory of having so recently the Prince of Wales as an undergraduate. What could the vicar say to mitigate his son's unmannerly behaviour? What painful discussions must have taken place, day after day, between Effie and himself. And what was now left for the vicar to look forward to?

Supposing it had been for something really worth while! But to become a reporter on a London newspaper! For Burr this was the final dishonour. From time to time a seedy little man, a reporter from the local paper, would call at the vicarage in search of some trifling paragraph. The little man was so timid, so ill-dressed, so absurd with his pencil and notebook, that the vicar, without malice, would make little jokes about him at tea-time. People like Burr and Effie did not like having their activities mentioned in the newspapers. It was vulgar to be discussed in public, though an exception might possibly be made in the case of the London *Times* or *Punch*.

The vicar never once mentioned to his son the sorrow he felt, and Robert remained equally silent, so that the rift was never quite mended. Though they remained politely affectionate to each other, neither was able sufficiently to appreciate what was good in the other. But when seven years later Robert brought me on the scene, Burr froze into an icy silence. I was the final insult. The foreign girl entering his gates!

The year 1921 saw Robert catapulted into world news. He had gone, with all the selfishness of his youth, unyieldingly about his business. His obstinacy, which was to serve me well at the time of our engagement, had allowed him in 1921 to hurt his parents without caring for the damage to their hidden feelings.

Since his early days at Eton, that is to say about 1915, Robert had spent his holidays wandering alone through the streets of London. Clearly he could not be expected to spend every day in contemplation before the Thames at the bottom of the garden. His parents had settled with all their books and treasures in the middle of a smoky area in which they had a multitude of needy parishioners but not a single friend. Effie, aware of this, allowed

74

her son to discover by himself the joys and sorrows of the immense metropolis, the heart of which, that is to say Hyde Park Corner, was only seven miles away.

Thus Robert, with an allowance of five shillings a day from Effie, would take a tram at the corner of Ealing Road and travel in it to Chiswick Park station, where the district railway would take him to Victoria or Charing Cross. If on the other hand he wanted to go to Dover Street or Piccadilly Circus, then he would change at Hammersmith and take the underground—the Piccadilly Line—which, in those days, had a guard between every two coaches whose business it was to manipulate the gates (they were not yet doors) when the train stopped at a station.

As his fares accounted for only a quarter of his allowance, he had more than enough to suffice his needs, all the more so because it would never have struck him to buy himself a meal, or even a cup of tea, being far too interested in imbibing the passing scene. This occupation may sound monotonous to those who have not developed a close affinity with the heart of great cities. At this stage his theatre-going was confined to the posters in the tube stations, and the exteriors of the theatres themselves, and there was really no need to see *Chu Chin Chow* or the Bing Boys when all the town was singing the tunes and when, at the beginning of each term at Eton, boys more favourably placed, and who had been taken by their parents to these shows, talked incessantly about them. At Eton also everybody read the *Bystander* and the *Tatler*, in which the theatrical and social events of the town were widely depicted and described. Already an immense love for London was beginning to run through Robert's veins, and by interminably plodding the streets he was developing that sense of lonely observation that made him so perfectly miserable when confined to close quarters.

After his departure from Magdalen, the visits to Henry Ainley at the St James's Theatre or any trip at his father's expense to the Continent came to an end. The war was over and he needed to free himself from dependence on Effie. Only a great national newspaper could bring the sort of freedom he desired. But even so he managed once again by his callousness to hurt.

A leading insurance company, anxious to discover a trainee

who could eventually become a partner, advertised in *The Times*. What perverse streak in Robert's character excited him to apply for the job? Nothing could have been less suitable. But it may have been a question of money. It is possible, though when I asked him he could not remember, that some tempting salary was mentioned, in which case he may have wished to impress his parents. Candidates were required to obtain a reference. Robert wrote to Dr Alington, his Eton headmaster, who had shown a great affection for him, and the reference must have been glowing because the company wrote to him saying that he had been chosen for the situation. Robert wrote back to say the post no longer interested him. He was going to try to get a job with the *Daily Express*. His action infuriated the board of the insurance company, who had turned down over four thousand candidates in his favour, and now found themselves in an absurd situation.

But possibly it had forced Robert to walk into the *Daily Express* one evening and ask for a job. He got it because Guy Pollock, the assistant editor, himself an Old Etonian, passing the waiting-room at that instant, saw him wearing an Old Etonian tie. 'There's no place for you here,' said Guy Pollock. 'You must get experience in the provinces before you come to London.' 'Take me on,' said Robert, 'and don't pay me till you are satisfied that I'm worth hiring.' 'Take you on when?' 'Tonight,' said Robert.

And so he was hired.

Things at Stacey Street were becoming difficult. By degrees Matilda was getting used to the idea that we would have to part. I also was miserable but with no clear idea of what to do. I was only gradually discovering threads in the complicated tapestry of Robert's background, never quite sure of what his parents thought of me, often frightened that he might not after all turn out to be the sort of husband I needed. I had never felt so desperately alone.

When at Stacey Street I woke up in the morning, I could not help being aware that Matilda had changed. She was tied up in knots, and there was not the same warmth in her voice. Usually so tender, so enveloping, she wrapped up her sorrow in hostility, and probably hated herself for doing it, as I hated myself for

hurting her. It seemed as if we were all hurting one another
When she was sulking, indulging in long silences, followed by
short, hurtful sarcasms, I turned to Nanny, our cat, who gave me
the same sort of understanding comfort as the pekinese did at
Brentford. Nanny got all the kisses that I secretly longed to give
my mother but dared not. In the same way that Robert appeared
to have no friends, or at least none sufficiently close to confide in,
so I had nobody to whom I could turn.

I began to enjoy my visits to Brentford, for come what might,
Effie provided me with the warmth and affection I so badly
needed. Besides, the slow unravelling of her fascinating stories
intrigued me. I was by nature an excellent listener and at poignant
moments my tears came easily. This trait in me surprised her but
rendered me, I fancy, more dear to her.

We nearly always found ourselves back in her Little Room.
She had a Madame Récamier *chaise-longue* that was doubtless
French, and this being in the centre of the room gave it almost
the impression of dividing it in two, but it served both to recline
on and also as a surface on which to pile her basket, her Bible,
and her various papers. There was also a tall screen of glass that
opened like a triptych and was framed in the prettiest wood
painted bright gold so that it matched the frames of the paintings
that hung from all the walls. This glass screen protected one from
draughts without hiding the view, and I thought it charming.
On my first visits I had rather imagined that Peli had confined her
water-colours to copies of Old Masters but this was far from the
case. She had copied religious subjects at Florence and Rome, as
Pope wrote verses in his youth in the style of other poets so that
he should gradually improve his technique until ready to create
one of his own. Many of these that hung in Effie's Little Room
now hang in mine to remind me of those visits to Brentford.
Delightful heads of Effie and her sister Helen when little, golden-
haired girls, as pure and blue-eyed as angels. A perfectly delightful
study of a pet squirrel eating an apple on the white linen table-
cloth of her home in Hans Place. She had left it to Effie with a
request that it should be given in due course to her grandson
Robert when he was old enough to appreciate it, and she had
added for his information: 'The poet Tennyson came to see me,

77

wishing to look at a drawing I had done of a squirrel; but he was disappointed because the squirrel was seated on the dinner-table, eating an apple on a white table-cloth and not on the branches of a forest tree.'

I had learnt to raise my voice a little when talking to Effie. This was not always easy for me, for I have a soft voice that does not carry. At lunch, Burr who had remained silent while I was saying something to Effie, suddenly broke in: 'You should raise your voice. My wife is a little deaf.' I had blushed dreadfully. I feared perhaps mistakenly, that his remark was uttered in a cold, hostile manner. I was by now sensitive to ill winds. They blew from so many quarters.

This warning gave me the excuse to tell Effie about my grand-mother at Blois, who was much deafer than she, but just because of that I loved her all the more; being obliged to be so patient with her increased my affection. And I added for Effie's amuse-ment: 'She lived in a sort of fairy-tale world in which she saw herself as a beautiful young woman galloping cross country seated side-saddle on a white horse.' Effie smiled delightedly. She liked me to tell her stories, and though she was a difficult person to converse with when there were people in the room, she was very easy as soon as there were just the two of us. Then her whole attitude became softer, more feminine. I found in her, I think, qualities that I had previously associated with mothers superior of convents—a blend of stern duty but immense inner understanding. Effie also had a gift for that routine which made of her, with her keys and attention to detail, especially with money, the soul of a well-run house.

At this moment she was seated on the Madame Récamier sofa, and she had asked me for her wicker basket with her Bible and her knitting. This she laid on her lap and after a little searching inside —there were so many things in it—drew out a small package done up in white tissue paper. She undid it very carefully, gradually re-vealing an exquisite pearl and gold Florentine brooch, and she said:

'I am not very sure of the exact origin of this beautiful thing but it has always been given to the young brides in my family— Hannah, the Rothschild girl, Blanche FitzRoy and me—the Lindsay girl. Now that you are to be my son's bride, I give it to you.'

5

I ASKED EFFIE how she had met Burr, and she told me that shortly after being presented at court she went to Mildmay in the north of London to become a deaconess. To Mildmay one summer went the vicar of Brentford in search of a deaconess to help in his parish. Effie met the clergyman over the parlour table and agreed to look into the proposition. An older deaconess took her to Brentford. The two women refused tea for fear of inconveniencing the bachelor cleric, and returned by river steamboat down the Thames from Kew Bridge. But Effie had already fallen in love.

But why in the first place had Effie gone to Mildmay? Was it out of revulsion for the sort of life that her mother, Peli, was leading as writer, painter, musician, hostess and patroness of the arts? The fact that Effie was deeply religious might not in itself have been enough for her to leave that sumptuous house in Hans Place, Knightsbridge, every morning to work amongst the poor in Islington or Mildmay. Peli herself was religious as indeed her own parents had been. As indeed were all the Lindsays, which did not prevent them from being soldiers, statesmen, politicians. But the fact is that Effie, in her own words, almost immediately after being presented at court, when her Rothschild cousins gave a great ball for her at their mansion in Piccadilly, went off to Islington and to Mildmay every day to work amongst the poor. And in the evening while Peli was entertaining William Morris, Burne-Jones or G. F. Watts, Effie would come back with mud on her skirts and fleas in her hair. One wonders what effect on Blanche her daughter's engagement to Burr must have had. And yet it was not possible to imagine a happier marriage than that between Effie and Burr. Looking back on it I am inclined to think that they were the two happiest people I have ever met. Perhaps the only completely happy people. The king in the story Blanche FitzRoy read when she was a girl of eleven in her schoolroom at Tours would have found in them what he was looking for—perfect content!

But there was somebody about whom Effie seldom spoke—her father, Sir Coutts, Uncle Bob's elder brother. You will recall that he left the Army to become an artist. Blanche also had met the man she was to marry shortly after her presentation at court and the beginning of her love affair was surrounded by the same bitter conflict, resolute opposition, that seemed to mark all those of the girls in this family, from Hannah onwards. But Blanche's was the only one that failed to end as happily as it began. For this reason Effie seldom spoke about her father.

Hannah at this time was a widow. The loss of her only son, Little Arthur, was a blow from which she never recovered. What mother ever completely recovers from the loss of an only son—an only son in childhood? Matilda, my own mother, never got over the loss of my baby brother from diphtheria. Much of the bitterness in her character was the direct result of it. A year later Hannah lost her husband but meanwhile Blanche had blossomed out into a beautiful woman. Though Hannah made a great effort to take her out that summer she knew that her strength was waning. The first dance she took her to was at Londonderry House, the second was at the Austrian Embassy, but after these two dances, Hannah's strength ebbed and Blanche was left much to herself. She once went to visit the studio of an artist who was painting the frescoes of Dorchester House. He was Sir Coutts Lindsay, and Blanche fell in love with him at first sight—just as her mother, Hannah, had fallen in love at first sight with Henry FitzRoy, to the scandal of both families.

As soon as they heard the news about Blanche, Hannah's family put forward objections. Not only was Sir Coutts twenty years older but he was living a dangerously free Bohemian life. He had models, one of whom he was known to be in love with. The more Blanche heard her suitor criticized, the more eager she became to marry him. And just as Hannah had married the man she loved so did Blanche marry Sir Coutts, who took her off to his castle of Balcarres in Fifeshire with its grey turrets rising above a rocky sea coast.

This was the castle in which Effie and her sister Helen spent much of their girlhood, so cold in winter that in order to wash in the morning they had to break the ice. But what was it like when Sir Coutts first took his bride there? Here is her first letter:

Balcarres,
Fife

My darling Mama,

    You cannot tell how often I think of you now, how tenderly and lovingly. I feel I have made a happy choice, and one which I do not think I shall ever have cause to regret, at least so far as human eyes can see, and I cannot help thinking that this must be a comfort to you, and that the peace of mind of my present life will be some consolation to you. My only trouble is about yourself. I cannot help fretting about your health and wishing that you might be better.

Should you desire me at any time to return to London do not hesitate to say so; not only if you are ill, I do not mean that; but if you want me, and think that your recovery would be quicker were I in London for a few days.

The people here welcome me and seem to be glad to see me. The place certainly wants furnishing and doing up, but not so much as you think. The grounds could hardly be improved and the view is wild and desolate. We paid two visits yesterday, and you are right when you fancy my pony carriage dashing. It is both dashing and comfortable—dark blue picked out with red; and red and blue rosettes on the horses' heads. I set out dressed in my blue silk dress with white stripes made by Madame Leblond, my silk jacket with tails, and my little hat with the peacock's feathers; Poole's railway wrapper with its white embroideries on a dark blue ground looked admirable.

We went first to Sir John and Lady Bethune, our nearest neighbours, who have a place something like Balcarres in architecture. Lady Bethune was at home and we were shown into a drawing-room much like any drawing-room in London. She came in—a small, round, dark-haired Frenchwoman about thirty, dressed in muslin with a blue belt, one curl on one shoulder and a household basket of keys and letters in her hand. She told me she had been married six years and could not get used to the thick leather boots and wool dresses worn by the country ladies. I sympathized for I hate heavy soles an inch thick and clinging woollen dresses. She laughed and said I must come to that however I might struggle against it.

Our next visit was to Sir Robert and Lady Anstruther who were also at home. They were very different people; he is the Member and a Liberal. A bright, gay young man, shewing excellent teeth. They have five children all of whom seemed to have an ardent desire to break their necks, running into all sorts of holes and corners. We went to the Scotch church, which is only two miles from here. It is a strange service and I had great difficulty in making out what the clergyman said. One needs no Prayer Book; the Minister prays what he pleases, and the people stand! They never kneel at all and sing sitting, listen to the Bible and the sermon sitting and stand during all the prayers.

We were obliged to return the visit of some amiable but peculiarly homely people whose name is Christie. I thought I should have been bored and should not have known what to do, but it turned out the reverse. The father is an old man who is proud of his garden and took us there. We ate some fruit. There were three daughters, one a widow, two unmarried and neither young nor beautiful, dressed astonishingly in pale cottons and brown holland! There was a piano, a harp and an organ in the drawing-room. One of the daughters played the organ by heart and well. They brought in some tea and pound cake, and the tea, as in story books, was served in large, old-fashioned cups with thick cream.

I see the gardener's wife every day. She went to Edinburgh to consult a surgeon, who took her into a large room with students all round. They stared at her and then pronounced her fate, telling her to return in a fortnight. She won my heart by saying that she knew what an only child was; she was one herself and she was sure that you and I must miss each other.

After lunch, the other day, instead of driving straight home we went to Elie and leaving our pony carriage, took a walk among the rocks, and on the sands, where it was sheltered. I sat down on Coutts' coat and watched the little waves lapping on the shore. There was not a soul to be seen anywhere; it is totally solitary and I do not know what you will say to me when I relate that I actually took my shoes and stockings off and holding my petticoats up (my tail and crinoline) in a most rustic way, danced about for a minute or two in the little wee waves at the edge of the sea!

We went to the dairy this morning. It is a clean room though the building is not picturesque. I mean it is not a poetical dairy but I lapped a little cream of which there were some large flat dishes all round. The laundry is pleasant; there are excellent presses and drying grounds.

I had a note last night from Lady Bethune asking us to dinner. We hired the one available fly in the neighbourhood, having nothing of our own but an open pony carriage. I arrayed myself in what I considered to be a most appropriate costume; a pale blue silk dress, low at the neck, with short sleeves and a long train. In my hair a couple of bunches of crimson carnations. As a bride I was taken in with due ceremony by the host, who carved the turbot and mutton himself, according to Scottish custom.

I have spent the greater part of the morning in the village of Collinsburgh. The air is fresh and pleasant and by a short cut in the park I can reach Collinsburgh in five minutes. There has been a great haul of herrings and the poor people buy two or three for a penny, and hang them up in rows outside their doors to dry, which looks picturesque and northern. Many of the men are whalers and on the road to church there is a cottage with two huge teeth of a whale forming a fierce looking arch. We met a regular Scotch girl; she was a milkmaid, I think, and wore good clothes with a tidy straw bonnet but she was barefoot, and you don't know how funny that looks!

Coutts has been trying to fish in the pond which is called a lake but after a while he gave it up, finding absolutely nothing, and rowed me about in a little boat called the Kingfisher.

Your loving daughter,

Blanche

They were soon back in London where they took a house in Grosvenor Square, where on the fifteenth day of May, 1865, Euphemia (Effie) Lindsay was born. Helen followed three years later. While Effie and Helen were growing up their parents became the pivot on which the artistic genius of the seventies in England was to turn. Painters such as Holman Hunt, G. F. Watts, Sir John Millais, Whistler, Rossetti and Edward Burne-Jones, gathered round them for a common purpose. Gilbert and Sullivan were to take the Grosvenor Gallery, the Lindsay's greatest venture, and work it into the theme of the opera *Patience*. It was on the nursery piano at Balcarres that Sir Arthur Sullivan composed the music for *The Sorcerer* while Effie and Helen played with their dolls. In London, the poet Browning became an intimate friend, wrote hundreds of letters to Blanche which Effie was to keep in neat bundles tied together with a ribbon, though as a girl of seventeen she was careful never to find herself alone in the same room. He had once chased her round a table and tried to kiss her while her mother looked on laughing.

Between the years 1862 and 1875 Sir Coutts exhibited ten pictures at the Royal Academy. During this period he saw that many fine artists were not represented at Burlington House. Having talked the matter over with Blanche they decided to build a place that, though not necessarily a rival to the Royal Academy, might accommodate the younger school of painters. Samuel Pratt, who owned an old curiosity shop at the corner of Maddox Street and Bond Street, said to Sir Coutts one day: 'If you are looking for a site to build a gallery, I know of a fine piece of ground.' 'Where?' asked Coutts. 'Here in Bond Street,' answered Pratt. 'If you're interested I'll take you round.' That was the start of the Grosvenor Gallery. Blanche threw all her talent into the decoration of the new building that was to rise in the heart of London's smartest shopping centre at a cost to Blanche of £120,000! Green marble was brought from Genoa to make the columns in the entrance hall. The ceiling was painted blue with gold stars. The wall panels were divided by Ionic pilasters, fluted with gilt, from the old Italian opera house in Paris. The walls themselves were entirely covered with deep crimson silk damask. As a prelude to its opening a great banquet was held in the main hall the food for which was prepared by Gounard, the Lindsays' French chef. Four of Queen Victoria's children were present: Edward, Prince of Wales, who was later to be King Edward VII; Princess Louise, who was to become the Duchess of Argyll; Prince Leopold, the future Duke of Albany, and the Duke of Connaught, whom Blanche had seen smacked by his royal mother twenty-five years before. Arthur Sullivan and Hallé were detailed to figure out who should take in whom to dinner. They had the most thankless job of all, for there were so many royalties and high-resounding names of every kind that it was pretty well past the wit of man not to make a blunder. The Rothschilds sent cartfuls of flowers from their estates of Gunnersbury and Mentmore, while Blanche arranged that her own gardener at Balcarres should send as many as he could. It was late when she arrived home to change for the banquet and she found countless notes requesting last-moment invitations. Her maid was frantic. Blanche was obliged to take her jewels in a heap and put them on as best she could in the carriage. The drive from Cromwell Place (where she and Sir Coutts were now living) is a tolerable distance. As she neared Piccadilly her teeth chattered and she turned cold. She was late, and a long string of carriages blocked the way. She had visions of her royal guests pacing up and down on the doorstep. The police, on hearing her name, cut the string of traffic and ten minutes later she flew up the stairs of the exhibition, to be told that the system of numbering had proved too much for Arthur Sullivan! The great musician had hardly begun to explain all the trouble when the Prince of Wales arrived.

The Prince took Blanche in to dinner, Sir Coutts took in Princess Louise, the Duke of Connaught escorted the Duchess of Teck. Fortunately for Sullivan and Hallé, guests sorted themselves out and all was well. Nevertheless Blanche sat trembling with nervousness until the Prince of Wales accidentally upset a glassful of champagne over her shoulder and sleeve, wetting her considerably and causing a great deal of laughter.

By ten o'clock the next morning the first guests streamed up the stairs. Whistler arrived with one white lock in his dark hair, prefacing every remark with the words: 'Don't you know, eh?' G. F. Watts advanced slowly in his long sealskin coat with a wisp of red ribbon showing at the neck, surrounded by the youngest and prettiest women in town. Robert Browning walked up with Augustus Sala, whose beaming face and world-famous white waistcoat gave him an air of dignity. Edward Burne-Jones let himself be seen in this place where his work was to unleash a torrent of abuse because he had the gift of never reading or listening to a single word of criticism.

Though my visits to Brentford became more frequent I was still working as a manicurist at the Savoy in the Strand. Robert and I had first met in the spring. We were now in September and I was beginning to feel the strain of having all this anxiety at a time when I was not very well.

One September evening when I had not been back to lunch because of the heavy rain, I returned home through Covent Garden with wet shoes and stockings splashed by the traffic. Matilda, as usual, was waiting for me but I could see that she was on edge. Our cat Nanny was asleep at the end of my couch. I went straight across the room to kiss her on the top of her soft, black head, and then I turned to my mother. Matilda braced herself and said, her lips tight and nervous: 'Is that all you've got to say to me?'

'What else can I tell you, except that it's been pouring with rain all day.'

'Well, if you have no news, I've got plenty. I've had a visit. Guess?'

'I haven't the faintest idea. Besides, I'm wet and tired.'

I did not need to question her. Matilda was incapable of keeping a secret. She always ended by blurting it out even if she were in a bad temper. Besides, who would it be but some new customer bringing her three yards of material to make a dress. My mother, annoyed by my lack of interest, exclaimed:

'Well, if you must know, I've had a visit from—your future mother-in-law!'

'What!' I cried in a sort of panic, my legs starting to give way under me. How was it that I had never foreseen the possibility of this frightening eventuality? And why did the very idea of it terrify me to this absurd extent? I sat down on the couch, and asked: 'Tell me—tell me everything!'

Matilda relaxed a little. I think she was glad to have frightened me and now she felt compassionate. She would enjoy telling me the whole story from the beginning.

'I heard the front door bell,' she said.

'And so?'

'I wrapped the front door key in a bit of old newspaper and was about to throw it out of the window, as I do for my customers, when I saw her hat, and it didn't look like the hat of anybody I knew, or indeed of any new customer who might be sent to me by an old one. The hat made me suspicious. Then, I saw that the woman in the hat was accompanied by somebody who might well be her daughter. So I withdrew my head quickly, closed the window and went downstairs. And then when I saw her features I guessed immediately who it was. Your fiancé is her very image. And it was obvious that the girl beside her was her daughter.

'They probably introduced themselves. I can't remember. At all events, what does it matter? I didn't need an introduction. Was I taken by surprise? Well, naturally. Who wouldn't be, and nervous also but ready to go over to the attack if it were to prove necessary, for how could I tell for what reason they had come? My first idea was that they had come to persuade me that it was time for you to break your engagement but I managed to keep my head and invite them politely to come up.

'When I opened the room door, I saw Nanny on her four paws at the end of your couch. Her neck was arched inquisitively but she hadn't hidden under the table, which she generally does when strangers arrive, and I took that as a good omen. I asked them to push Nanny aside and sit on your couch as everybody does when they come to visit us. They had no choice anyway. There's nowhere else for guests to sit.

'They didn't seem very sure whether to talk in French or in English but as they appeared to speak both languages indifferently, we remained in this respect on strictly neutral ground. Clearly they had *not* come as ambassadors-extraordinary. They carried no ultimatum and were merely here to spy the country out, anxious to see into what sort of a noose your Robert was sticking his head. This being so, I really had nothing to worry about.

I couldn't change what had obviously hit them in the eye, that we lived in a shabby one-room apartment. If they didn't like it that was just too bad for them. However ardently I might pray for a miracle I couldn't change the room into a town house in Mayfair.

'Fortunately Nanny did her stuff. She climbed on the girl's lap and began arching her back and purring, and when I asked your future mother-in-law if she would like a cup of tea, she answered: "Oh, yes, Madame Gal, I would love one!" Her enthusiasm put me at ease right away.

'I decided to serve tea in the best cups—the ones with the blue flowers from the tea service you bought me last year at the Haymarket Stores when you were working at that poky little barber's shop in Coventry Street. I had a struggle finding the saucers, which we ordinarily never use, so as to economize in the washing up. Yes, I know. I found them in the end but I was in such a panic I scarcely knew what I was doing. Fortunately I had remembered to put some pennies in the gas-meter and the kettle was soon on the boil.

'After your future mother-in-law had drunk her tea, she said: "Madeleine tells me that you have only just recovered from a bad attack of sciatica which kept you in bed for several weeks. Oh! How I pity you! I myself suffer terribly from rheumatism, and living so near the Thames is just the opposite of what I should do. Fancy! The tide flows at the bottom of our garden, and sometimes comes up right to the walls of the house. Madeleine says that at Clichy you were virtually on the towing-path of the Seine. What an extraordinary coincidence the two children growing up in similar circumstances!"

'The sound of your name on her lips went straight to my heart. Yes, it was lovely to hear her saying: "Madeleine this . . ." and "Madeleine that . . ." as if she had always known you. Really, it was the sweetest thing she could possibly have said but, oh, what a chatterbox you must be! What made you talk to her about my sciatica? As if she really cared.

'You should have seen her, sitting with her daughter, on the edge of your couch with Nanny going from one to the other, purring. She said:

"I wonder if you would mind if I took my hat off? I get a

88

headache when I wear it too long, and it prevents me from hearing what you say. I am slightly deaf."

'She smiled, as if excusing herself for having this physical defect, and added:

"Madeleine tells me that your dear mother—Madeleine's grandmother from Blois—was even deafer than I am?"

'Oh, much more so!' I exclaimed. 'She was so deaf that I was sometimes obliged to take her head between the palms of my hands and yell into her ear!'

Matilda laughed.

'Who would have believed,' she said, 'that only five minutes after first meeting your future mother-in-law I should be discussing my family at Blois as if we had known each other all our lives! I almost felt as if I had fallen into a trap. It was too good to be true.

'But guess what I was doing all this time? I was fascinated by the strands of silky white hair resting against cheeks still fresh and youthful—and those lovely hands of hers with her rings with the sapphires and emeralds encircling her fingers! I have never seen anything so beautiful outside the windows of the big jeweller's in the Rue de la Paix—but on hands like hers they looked infinitely prettier.

'She said that my tea was excellent. She even asked for a second cup. That really won my heart. Of course, I could see that she was terribly tired. The journey from Brentford by tram and tube must have exhausted her. Besides, she must have been nearly as nervous as I was. Although, of course, one could tell that she was a woman who had never worked for her living—at least not like us. A real clergyman's wife, in short. That's why I kept on the defensive. Mme Maroger, the pastor's wife at Clichy, was like that—at home anywhere, whether it was a palace or a pigsty—polite, amiable, always knowing just what to say. But how can one be sure what's in their heads? And now, I ask you! What's going to happen to us? To you and to me? I swear I believe that Robert will never marry you!'

All this left me wretchedly perplexed. My imagination had never pictured a meeting between Effie and Matilda, and now I just did not know what to think of it. In a village, of course, everybody would know everybody, and this sort of thing might not be necessary, but at the thought of Effie with her white hair making the long journey from Brentford especially to see Matilda, I not only felt ashamed but a shiver of apprehension ran up my spine. Matilda said:

'The girl was pink-cheeked and fresh—the same blue eyes, well brought up, and speaking only when she was spoken to, but how she looked! How she looked at everything. Her opinion will be damning.' Then with clinical objectivity: 'But, after all, why should we care? It is not you who are chasing the young man but the young man who is running after you!'

The last words were spoken harshly as she banged the hot iron on the damp seam of a dress she was ironing. The tight seam screeched like a poor bird wounded by some cruelly hard object. My heart beat savagely against my ribs. I would not go out this evening unless, of course, Robert called for me.

He did call for me, and we went out to supper but because of the troubled state of my mind, I was aggressive. What had he done after getting that job on the *Daily Express* in the autumn of 1921? Why did I not know more about the life he had led during the last six years?

There was nothing in what he had done, he said, to prove that he was capable of giving me the sort of life that I wanted. Being on a great newspaper, at a time when there was no other method for the dissemination of news—not even sound radio—was immensely exhilarating, but what had he got to show for it? Very little. On the *Morning Post*, since the General Strike, and Winston Churchill editing the *British Gazette* in their office, he had run into a dull spell. On the other hand his adventure with me was sufficiently exciting to occupy pretty well the whole of his attention. Being in love was something that he had no intention of taking lightly.

Had 1921 been an important year for him?

Yes, he said, but he had shown from the beginning a positive genius for picking wild flowers at the side of the road instead of keeping his eyes on the things that really mattered.

For instance?

The things he remembered best were those that really did not matter at all. Like Fleet Street as it was then, still with drays and horse-drawn delivery vans with a boy and a dog behind, the boy swinging like a monkey from the knotted rope suspended from the roof so that he should not fall out; the tricycle boys whistling the latest musical comedy hit, the slow taxis, paper-boys racing along the pavement with a pile of late-extras under an arm and the contents bill flapping against their frayed trouser ends. 'All the winners! Lady X Divorce sensation.'

'What else?'

The ever repeated excitement of turning into Shoe Lane, narrow and smelling of horse dung, hot chocolate cake, printers' ink and those five-miles-long rolls of newsprint being unloaded by chains and a pulley from stationary lorries—and then the run up the wide stone stairs into the immense barn-like editorial room with its high, dusty windows, bare walls and yellow pillars on which R. D. Blumenfeld, then editor, stuck his list of Do's and Dont's for reporters and sub-editors. Don't use the word very. Don't split an infinitive. Put all the guts of your story in the first paragraph. (This was so that the rest of it could be progressively cut if space were required for fresh news in subsequent editions.)

Atmosphere! That was what he enjoyed. Running hither and thither about London as dusk fell or at night under the street lamps on this story, then on that one. No cars to carry reporters swiftly and blindly to their destinations. They used public transport or their legs. They were precipitated into a swift succession of human dramas between tea and bedtime, absorbing the way other people lived, financiers on the run, an actress in her dressing-room, the birth of a baby in a bus in Peckham. Like an impressionist painter capturing the homely scenes of a great capital, like being paid to do what he had done on holidays from Eton while searchlights probing for raiding German Zeppelins criss-crossed the night sky of the London he loved.

There had been no union to prevent Guy Pollock from allowing Robert to prove his worth. Nothing the first week, one pound the second, and then an extra pound every subsequent week till he reached what was then the minimum of nine pounds. Nine pounds backed by gold. The banks would still with a little persuasion hand one warm, golden sovereigns. But his salary was paid by a cheque on the firm, which many cashed at the sausages-and-mashed potatoes counter of the long, narrow shop at the corner of Shoe Lane and Fleet Street, while sitting on a high stool in front of a tureen filled with sizzling fried onions. He need have no qualms about returning to Brentford in the small hours of the morning. He had a job. Work had its privileges. The vicar had been almost shocked by what his son could earn in a despised profession so quickly after slamming the door on Magdalen. It was more than the vicar had ever earned. But Effie, on Burr's instructions, still would not trust him with a latch-key. He was so careless, and the vicar was terrified of burglars and fire. At 2 a.m., sometimes later, Robert would knock at the heavily barred front door at the bottom of the slope, ashamed of having to bring down Effie in her nightdress under a Jaeger dressing-gown, her lovely white hair tied by a ribbon in her nape, the tortoise-shell combs all out of it, her features drawn with tiredness. He had once again destroyed her chance of a good night's sleep. But was it his fault? Pitiless, with nothing but a peck on her lovely soft forehead to thank her for her pain, he would brush past her up to his room. Effie would return wearily to hers, careful not to wake up Burr, and slipping into her side of the great old-fashioned bed, cry softly while Burr in his vast white linen nightshirt snored.

At the office there were two shifts—one from morning to evening, the other from afternoon to night. But nobody would have dreamt of breaking off from a story because it was time to go home. Out-of-town assignments could take one anywhere—big cities or some sleepy old English village where the yokels gathered at the local pub and bed and breakfast at the hotel cost 3s. 6d. One might come home the same evening after phoning one's story, or have to remain there for two or three days—a week, perhaps. So that, as the vicarage had no telephone, news could only be sent there by telegram (which was unthinkable) or by letter. On most occasions Robert was unable to warn Effie that he had gone out of town and would not be back that night. So from midnight onwards she would wait for him patiently till at dawn she finally consented to close her eyes. Imagine the weariness and anxiety of her vigil. But what was all this to him—dazzled by excitement and colour?

The Big Room at the *Daily Express* was arranged in this manner.

Up against the tall windows facing south and west was the horseshoe table of the sub-editors. At the head of it sat the grumbling, white-haired chief sub-editor. After the day shift he was replaced by the night-editor. Sub-editors dealt with the news that went into the paper. Their title was misleading. They were modest and hard-worked, humble men for the most part, grey about the temples, experienced and phlegmatic, the very opposite of a junior reporter's youthful ardour, lack of experience and impetuosity.

As news came in, faster and faster as afternoon turned to evening, from the ticker tapes of the various agencies, such as Reuters and the Central News, from the news editor and from the telephonists taking at dictation the stories being phoned back to the office by reporters both in and out of town, or even by members of the public who knew that they would get paid for a quick piece of information, the chief sub-editor would glance at each item, and having marked on it the headline he wanted, would toss it over to the sub-editor he thought most capable of dealing with it. He in turn would clip the English, cut it to size, re-write it if necessary, and invent a snappy title. This in itself was a work of art for which experience was vital. The snappy head-line of a very short news item could often, by its wit or cleverness, 'make' a page. What the chief sub did not want, he spiked, just as the sub-editors spiked every single sheet of paper they no longer wanted, in case there might later be a dispute about the copy. The copy itself, in its finished state, was sent back to the chief-sub's desk for his approval, after which he would send it up to the printers, either by the compressed air chute, as bills in old-fashioned drapers' shops, or by an office boy. Meanwhile the still damp proofs of material from the 'stone' would ceaselessly arrive. The first edition was taking shape.

The part of the Big Room between the sub-editors' horseshoe table and the far end was occupied by padded telephone booths where the operators took copy being phoned in, and by several rows of reporters' desks which had lately become rather elegant, in varnished wood with typewriters attached, and which folded in when not in use. They could be bought by a reporter for a modest sum retained each week out of his salary cheque. Here also sat the Woman Editor with her staff, a compact department of her own though not separated from the rest of the room by anything that marked its frontiers other than in one's imagination. At the far end of the room by the east window were the newspaper files, with all the various editions of the paper as they were published throughout the night, so that if a story published in a country edition had been killed before the London editions one could trace it without difficulty. Here also was the news editor's small boarded-off room in which sat the famous J. B. Wilson, with his bald head and eternal pipe, the only journalist who had been on the *Daily Express* before Lord Beaverbrook, who owned it, had first arrived in England from Canada. All the morning J. B. Wilson, with an enormous pair of scissors in his hand, would go through the rival morning papers, more especially the *Daily Mail*, to see what stories he might have missed or what stories they had which he felt might be usefully followed up. In due course he would repeat the operation with the evening papers as they arrived in his office. Meanwhile his secretary would be busy taking calls not only from members of the staff out on their assignments and asking for instructions but from every source from which news first mysteriously took shape. Then one would see J. B. Wilson opening the door with a great clatter, and striding out to hand a letter, or a note, or a newspaper clipping, to some waiting reporter whom he thought most fitted to deal with it.

To the left of the way in to the Big Room was the waiting-room to which callers were sent up by the porter in Shoe Lane—a man who had witnessed an accident in the Strand or somebody who disagreed with the sentiments expressed in a leader on the leader page.

At 5 p.m. the Big Room would start to warm up. Those writing early stories at their desks would send out for a pot of tea and hot chocolate cake from the tearoom in Shoe Lane, all beautifully served on a clean tray, the chocolate cake made by the women who owned the place and always warm, just out of the oven, and the whole thing for 1*s*. 6*d*. and a tip of 3*d*. for the boy who brought it up. And then towards 6 p.m. everything would spring to life for

94

the editorial conference at which the editor and the heads of all the different departments, J. B. Wilson, the news editor, the leader writers, the foreign editor, the chief sub-editor, would plan the appearance, as far as events permitted them, of the paper and what must be said in the leaders.

Then, as the day staff went home, and the night staff alone remained, the Big Room would settle down to a warm, gentle throb, as of a great liner pursuing its way quietly across the ocean, with the engines purring in the engine-room and often the distinguished figure of R. D. Blumenfeld in evening dress with a flower in his lapel, sitting at a plain deal table against the north wall, all by himself, facing the busy, almost silent expanse in front of him, as he looked thoughtfully at the large square damp pull of the front page of the 11 p.m. edition. He had dined in the company of the Prince of Wales. He would be talking to Lord Beaverbrook on the telephone. After the owner, he was the captain in charge of the ship. He was master of the crew's immediate destinies.

How small, and yet how memorable, were Robert's first assignments, not perhaps his first but those which he liked to talk about—a dispute between the London County Council and the Metropole in Northumberland Avenue, who had put on a supper show called The Midnight Follies. One needed to imagine the primness of London in those days immediately following the end of the 1914–18 war to hear without surprise that he was sent, evening after evening, to see for how long the hotel would be allowed to go on with its attempt to brighten up the town by instituting a supper entertainment of the cabaret type which 'is so popular in Paris, New York, and other great cities of the world'. In fact what was at stake was the whole spirit of D.O.R.A. (the Defence of the Realm Act) which had dampened down entertainment while the troops were fighting in the trenches.

Here, in a way, Robert must have re-discovered something of the atmosphere he had found a year earlier at the St James's Theatre when Henry Ainley had allowed him to come whenever he liked behind the scenes both during *Peter Pan* and a straight play he was producing at the same time. But this was younger, brighter, altogether more exciting, and everybody in the company from the directors to the girls in the chorus were anxious to show their gratitude to the representatives of great London newspapers championing their cause. Here then he felt for the first time the prestige that surrounds even the newest, youngest, least important reporter on a world-famous paper. Last night he was nobody. Tonight he is carried on the shoulders of fame. He is powerful, he is a million sale, he is a press lord by proxy. If he can move the public by his pen, he has the means of saving the jobs of a troupe of forty players.

A short time before the show was due to begin he would jump on a bus and ride as far as Trafalgar Square. The paper was experimenting with a device on the top of a high building for spelling out short news bulletins by electric bulbs which gave the impression of a continuous stream of information. Though few people stopped to take advantage of it, this attempt to break new ground reflected a ceaseless urge to make the public share its youthful enthusiasm. Robert would stand on the steps of the National Gallery and gaze upwards at the slow-running lit-up commentary. Radio was not yet commercial. There were amateurs with crystal sets but when one evening he was sent a little way out of town to see if an experimental broadcast of voice news could carry far, nothing had happened. He had remained till past midnight vainly straining his ears for the agreed *Daily Express* signal.

The glamour of the theatre lasted a little longer until, in turn, it was submerged in Robert's impressionable mind by the more colourful and more vital happenings that took place in the world all about him—the University of the Street packed with more wisdom than is to be found in any college cloister. But it so happened that one day J. B. Wilson gave him, as a kindness, a season's press pass for the Russian Ballet Season at the old Alhambra, which ran from November to December of that year, 1921. It was perhaps one of the finest ballet seasons that London was ever to witness, with such dancers as Spessiva, Trefilova, Lopokova, Nemchinova, Woizikowsky and Tchernicheva. Here, he rediscovered all that had so enchanted him in the fairy-tales of those coloured books edited by Andrew Lang, which his Rothschild cousin, Uncle Leo, had given him as a child. The red plush orchestra stalls of the famous theatre in Leicester

Square, which had seen so many young soldiers in uniform on leave from the trenches during the war, added romance to the setting. But for some extraordinary reason, nobody went. The stalls were practically empty. Every night Robert would try to find a few minutes between assignments, sometimes when he was supposed to be on them, to watch passages from the *Boutique Fantastique*, *Le Lac des Cygnes*, *The Sleeping Beauty* and *Casse-Noisette*, to soak himself in the music of Tchaikovsky. He would present his press pass at the door and be shown to the stalls, where he would remain entranced—as the mad King of Bavaria must have been in his lakeside castle listening to Wagner's operas being performed for him alone! The minutes would fly. There would be something to be inquired into at Brixton or at Streatham Hill. A train must be caught at Victoria. A telephone call would have to be put through to the night editor. Did he dare remain five minutes longer? What was it that temptation was already whispering into his ear?

During these months vital events were taking place that never even penetrated his mind. Aware of small dramas, deliciously absorbed by a continual flow of criss-cross journeys across London to satisfy the exigencies of J. B. Wilson's prodigiously fertile imagination, politics and foreign affairs remained for him indigested on the front page. Europe was once more in turmoil, Ireland sinking into anarchy, Germany and Austria bankrupt and hungry. In Britain unemployment was rising. Before being thrown into the maelstrom, he would have been wiser to discover the reasons for all this discontent and unhappiness. He allowed himself to be plunged into the bubbling waters like a fool or an innocent.

One evening when all was still in the Big Room but the ticking of the clock and the scratching of pens and pencils on the sub-editors' horseshoe table, R. D. Blumenfeld beckoned him over. He said that there had been trouble on the Ulster Boundary and that a senior reporter who had been asked to go over to Ireland to cover the latest fighting had asked to be excused on the ground that after being three years in the trenches in France he had no desire to risk his life any more. 'Would you be willing to go?' asked R. D. Blumenfeld.

'When?' asked Robert.

'Tonight. There is a boat-train leaving in half an hour. I'll see if I can find somebody else to go with you.'

North and South, not satisfied with the terms of the Irish Treaty signed in December, while Robert's mind had been so engrossed by the Russian Ballet at the Alhambra, were resorting to force. Representatives of Southern Ireland were claiming large transfers of land, and Sir James Craig, Prime Minister of Ulster, hurried to London to consult with Winston Churchill and other members of the Irish Committee of the Cabinet. Almost at the same time, a new session of Parliament opened, and Mr Lloyd George made it clear that this boundary problem must be relegated to the comparatively distant future. But, earlier on this particular morning, the ticker had announced that Sinn Féin raiders had attacked the border counties of Fermanagh and Tyrone, kidnapping some Unionists, Orange leaders and magistrates. Michael Collins, Premier of the Irish Free State, came out with a statement that these raids were probably reprisals because some Sinn Féiners were to have been executed in Ulster. By now, that is to say, by evening, the situation was beginning to look serious. But how could Robert warn his mother?

On the Saturday morning in Belfast, they looked for something to cable home but there was really nothing. In a way, it did not matter because there would be no *Daily Express*—only the *Sunday Express* but, after all, it was their business to serve both newspapers. There had been a spot of bother at Monaghan. Robert offered to ride down on the day train to see what was happening. It sounded a good way of seeing the lush Irish countryside. The train arrived at Clones at 5.30 p.m. where it was to change engines. At the rear of the train were two carriages of 'B' specials, armed with rifles, and as the first men trooped out on the platform they were told by members of the Republican Army who were in possession of the station to surrender. Somebody opened fire and in the *mêlée* a Republican officer was killed. Seeing this, his men started to shoot indiscriminately. A hail of bullets swept through the carriages and with a shattering of glass four of the constabulary who remained inside were shot dead in their seats. This was Robert's baptism of fire. He was wise enough instead of running out on the platform, to open the opposite door and dive out onto the permanent way, where he lay on the centre track until the shooting was over. Unfortunately, retracing his journey as far as Monaghan, which in his ignorance he supposed north of the Border line and which in fact was south of it, he found an open post office with just ten minutes before it closed, and filed to London too picturesque an account of the station battle, proud to think he might hit the front page of the *Sunday Express*. The post office clerk, before sending the cable, asked Robert if he really wished to file it. She was trying to tell him that Monaghan was the headquarters of those very men who had shot and killed the 'B' specials, and that they would assuredly take swift reprisal upon him for suggesting that they had been murdered in their seats at the back of the train before they could take up their rifles. Robert refused to cancel the cable but wisely phoned Belfast to say where he was and what he had done. Then he walked across the road to the station hotel. It was too late by now to continue his journey. That night he was arrested and condemned to death by the Colonel of the Republican Army. But meanwhile his colleague in Belfast had got into touch with London and representations were made both to Winston Churchill and Michael Collins. All ended well and he was released and sent back to Belfast. But the *Daily Express* splashed the story of his adventure over the front page of its Monday morning issue so that he was (largely due to his naïve inexperience) catapulted from obscurity into fame, and marked out for great opportunities.

But what of Effie?

About 9.00 p.m. on the Sunday night, having as yet no inkling of why her son had not come back to sleep, she heard a loud knocking at the front door. Sunday was an exhausting day for the vicar and his wife. Now that they were old, they tried on Sundays to go to bed early. They had put out the lights downstairs and locked, barred and chained the door as was their custom. Burr was in bed and Effie had let down her beautiful hair and was brushing it. The knocking at the door gave her a start. 'There he is at last!' she said, putting on her dressing gown.

She took a lighted candle with her, went downstairs and went through her usual routine with the chains and the locks. Instead of her son there stood in front of her a young man called Ketchum, a clever young Canadian journalist recently hired by Lord Beaverbrook, who planned to give him big opportunities on the *Daily Express*. He looked at Effie, asked her who she was and then said, as if he were announcing the most joyful tidings: 'Your son has been condemned to death in Ireland. Can you lend us a photograph of him to put in the paper!'

Effie felt the blood draining away from her already white features. She had been tortured during the long last months of the war, knowing that unless it ended soon it would claim her son, and that this sort of thing might happen one day—a telegram or a message to say that he was wounded or dead.

'Is he dead?' she asked.

The young man in his well-cut overcoat looked at her ghostlike figure holding the lighted candle, and had sudden pity on her:

'Oh, no,' he said gently. 'He's on his way back to London. Tomorrow morning you'll find his story all over the front page.'

'I see,' said Effie trying to understand. Then she added: 'I think you'd better come in for a moment. I'll make you a cup of tea.'

6

THERE WAS THE loveliest water-colour of Effie at the age of eleven which Blanche Lindsay exhibited at the opening of the Grosvenor Gallery in 1877. It shows her standing in a white nightdress against a bowl of flowers, her blue eyes looking innocently out of the gilt frame.

It hangs in my bedroom and I am always surprised how easily I rediscover the features of my mother-in-law when old in this painting of her as a little girl. One afternoon when we were in her Little Room at Brentford, she said:

'Today I am the age that Peli was when she died, and this affects me deeply. Not that I fear death as such. I was taught to believe that it was the prelude to something else, and I continue to think so. No, it's not that. I want to go on living for a few more years in order to look after Burr. He could never manage without me.'

I smiled but she looked at me as if asking to be understood.

'You must sometimes think me very dull company, and my conversation unsuited to all the gay plans in your blonde little head. I have always had this dour, Scottish strain. It's a great handicap. When Robert was on his holidays from Eton I once tried to make him join me every morning in reading a chapter from the New Testament in Greek. It's such a lovely language, and he would have been a great help. He had been enchanted by Homer. But one morning he told me that I was trying to ram so much religion down his throat that I would end by putting him off it altogether. Do you think he really meant it? I have been desperately unhappy ever since.'

'We all say things like that to our mothers,' I said, 'and spend the rest of our lives regretting it.'

'Yes,' she agreed, 'but he did say it.'

She laughed.

'My mother had a theory,' she said, 'that instead of celebrating our birthdays we should all look forward to our death-days. On one of her birthdays, she wrote a poem that she published in a little book called *The Flower Seller*. I learnt it by heart.'

She recited:

When is my Death-day, solemn dreaded hour,
That gives no yearly witness I must die,
And, rent in fiercest fight, shall swooning lie
While Nature, pitiless, claims back her dower?
Each of us, on Life's tree, is but a flower
Whose wind-blown petals lean to earth or sky
As we toward mean or lofty conquest try—
Though some are plucked in bud for angels' bower.

'She wrote a lot of verse?' I asked.

'She wrote a lot of everything. She even did a little journalism, as you would call it today though the term might have shocked her. She wrote for a periodical called *Aunt Judy's Magazine* a series of short stories about a little girl called Lizzie (one of her own names was Elizabeth) in which she embodied many of her childish recollections. In Lizzie's father "Mr Roy" can be traced a vivid impression of my grandfather, Henry FitzRoy. My sister, Helen, copied out some of the passages:

'"Lizzie's father seemed to be scarcely older than herself; he was so full of fun and joyousness; his merry laugh came more readily even than hers; his jokes were as childish as her own. Lizzie knew what a busy life he led; being a statesman, he was usually out all day at his office in Whitehall, and he passed nearly every night in the House of Commons. Even during the brief space that he managed to spend at home he was liable to be often interrupted by a messenger, who brought one of those leather boxes whereon, in gilt letters, were stamped the words, "On Her Majesty's Service"—boxes that Lizzie hated cordially, as their arrival put an end to whatever game of romps happened to be going on, and generally even caused her dismissal from the library.

'"Time went on and Lizzie grew older, perhaps a trifle wiser.

Alas! when she was fifteen, her father caught a fever and died. A little while before his death on the morning of her birthday, she received from him a letter, for he was then staying in the country. The letter began as follows:

'"So my little girl has grown into a young woman of fifteen. I was in no hurry to lose my little playfellow, but I suppose it must be. The only thing in which I wish her to be a woman in self-control, and an effort to keep down temper when tempted. She cannot do this in her own strength, but I know she will pray for power to do it, for her old father's sake. May God bless you, my little Pet."

'Years have come and gone since that beloved letter was written but Lizzie reads it still from time to time. The ink is yellowing with age, and the folds of the paper are worn and soiled; yet as she cons the tender words written by the dear dead hand, her old childish love and devotion arise in her as strongly as ever, and an inexpressibly great longing surges over her heart and soul.

> But O for the touch of a vanished hand,
> And the sound of a voice that is still.

'Perhaps journalism is in the family,' I said. 'It is amusing to think of her as a young woman reporter—a reporter of her own inmost sentiments.'

My mother-in-law laid down the paper.

'Yes,' she said, 'I'm afraid you are landing yourself amongst a race of scribblers.'

My mother-in-law had been to London the previous day, all alone as was her custom, to buy a thing or two at Harrods, to walk down Bond Street past the Irish Linen shop, Roberts, the chemist, and several other places which had existed when she was a girl and had accompanied her mother in the carriage. In those days there were shopwalkers who bowed to Peli and her daughter and escorted her ladyship to the counter. But things had changed; nobody much recognized Effie any longer, and as she was about to cross Wigmore Street . . .

'I must tell you,' said Effie, to her daughter-in-law: 'I had been to Wigmore Street to have new spectacles made for me, but on the point of recrossing the road, the traffic had become so intense that I was terrified. So as I stood on the edge of the pavement, I prayed. I prayed that somebody would take pity on me. When I pray, I close my eyes. So I was standing there praying, with my eyes shut, when suddenly I felt a hand at my elbow. A very young man, a delightfully good-looking young man, was saying gently: "Don't be afraid. We will cross the street together, and you'll see. Everything will be quite all right." I was delighted. I could feel the blood colouring my cheeks with gratitude. How charming young people can be!'

As Effie said these words the sun came out from behind the trees of Kew Gardens on the far side of the river and it lit up her lovely face so that her blue eyes, the same vivid blue eyes as her son's, sparkled. The same sun touched the diamonds nestling against the gold seashells of her ear-rings. My mother-in-law had a passion for ear-rings and one seldom saw her without a favourite pair. These in the form of seashells were not only studded with diamonds but each had a large pearl in the centre. Perhaps they were Florentine like my brooch. Her ears were pierced but she would take off her ear-rings and put them on again with great speed, with the same swift, delicate movements as she employed when changing the rings on her fingers. Her coquettishness with her family jewels, those that had been worn by her mother and her grandmother, was most endearing and gave her a touch of charming femininity to counterbalance her occasional air of severity—though this was by no means her only feminine quality. She was as jealous as any other woman, and deep in her heart infinitely tender. As for her hair, it was always faultlessly arranged, and I own today an immense collection of the loveliest tortoise-shell combs, some encrusted with turquoises or rubies, which all came from the women who were her forbears.

'Oh!' she exclaimed suddenly. 'I have another little present for you!'

She went over to a very beautiful old English chest of drawers which had doubtless been Peli's, and from the bottom drawer she brought out cradled in her open palms long panels from the skirt and bodice of what must once have been a superb ball dress of richly flowered embroidered silk, the gold and silver threads weighing down the material. As she unwrapped each panel from its tissue paper I gave a cry of admiration. I suddenly remembered the description of the dress that Hannah had worn at the ball in Paris graced by the King and Queen of the French, in the course of which she had danced twice with Prince Edmond de Clary, who had fallen so desperately in love with her at first sight—a dress of white satin trimmed with small red roses. Who had worn this one and when? After Peli's death, the dress had been unstitched and the panels laid out between tissue paper for this long sleep in which they had remained almost forgotten, but not quite, for so many years.

'As your dear mother is so clever with her needle,' said Effie, 'and as you are likely to go out a great deal in the evening with my son, I thought you might like to have a ball dress which Peli once wore. It will be as if you were bringing her back to life again. The world is like that. The women of a family change and yet remain alike. I fear that my mother must have suffered from my distaste for balls and theatres, and yet I find myself increasingly close to her in thought, and I have no doubt that Robert will carry on in the tradition of his forbears. You will look very pretty in Peli's ball dress. May you inherit her artistic gifts!'

'That would be my greatest wish,' I said.

I had bought a rather amusing box of chocolates in a shop in Old Compton Street. It was round and the top was made like a French sailor's hat with a pompon in bright red. I hoped it might amuse Burr.

We were all three—Effie, Burr and myself—on the landing leading down to his study, and I was feeling rather ashamed of the futility of my gift. I offered it to Burr, telling him that it might remind him of those cross-Channel trips he once took from Folkestone to Boulogne. He seemed pleased. And when anything amused him the whole of his face took on an almost boyish grin. While I was making this gift, my mother-in-law was standing just behind me, up against the oak chest which was about the only piece of furniture in the hall, but so large that the children used to hide in it when they played hide-and-seek, until Effie had told them the story of the little girl who, having once hidden in just such a chest, could not lift up the lid again and was not found until she was dead.

Burr was trying to thank me for this absurd box of chocolates, but there still remained between us that uncomfortable coldness that came from the fact he was disappointed with his son and put some of the blame on me, doubtless because he felt that a rich girl, a girl from an old English family, would have known better how to bring the young man back into the ways of a dignified former Magdalen undergraduate. And I fancy that my mother-in-law was troubled to find herself increasingly taking my side. The mother-in-law, daughter-in-law bond was beginning to be very strong, and now truly I could say as Ruth said to Naomi: 'Entreat me not to leave thee . . .'

Well, suddenly I felt in the small of my back my mother-in-law's hand gently pushing me forward. I thought it might be a mistake, but no, the pressure increased, as if she were imploring me to do something. In a flash I understood. She was asking me to deposit a kiss on Burr's forehead. This I did, and turning round I saw the rather pathetic smile of gratitude on Effie's gentle features.

My troubles were far from over. My health, which had deteriorated all through the summer, now took a more serious turn. In spite of the relative luxury of the Savoy barber's shop, to spend long hours below street level was in direct contradiction to everything the doctors prescribed for me. Unless I stopped work immediately they feared for my life, they told my mother. What I needed was a warmer climate, complete rest and meals at regular hours. Their verdict spelt disaster. Matilda, all too aware of the danger, was at her wits' end. She had already experienced the irremediable tragedy of losing a child, and panicked at the thought of losing me. But it was no easy matter for her to suggest that I should leave the Savoy, which was not only the job in which I had been really happy but also it had been the best paid— sufficiently well paid to keep us both, and even allow us to put a little money aside, not much but nearly £100, with which we had started a banking account. If I left the Savoy our means of subsistence would disappear. She was earning less and less money as a dressmaker.

Neither of us could expect Robert to see things as we did. He was charming, undoubtedly in love but incapable of understanding problems that were outside the limits of his own world. 'Don't worry,' he said. 'Six months in some warm, dry place and you'll be well again,' His words sounded reassuring but they just didn't make sense. If something happened to him, Effie would be at his side with her well-run house and her cheque book. But though we were engaged, and I wore a ring, imagine what would be said if somebody suggested that there might be something really serious with my lungs. Which, of course, there was definitely not, for the moment, but who could tell what the future held in store? And Robert would not wish to boast about that sort of thing to his parents after such a lot of work trying to persuade them that I was the ideal bride! Just think how Burr would be bound to say that he had guessed it from the start—not only a foreign girl, a Roman Catholic suspiciously turned Protestant but dying, to boot!

Matilda saw herself alone once more—alone with me in a faintly unfriendly world, a world surrounded with dangers—with some insidious malady gnawing into my side—which, incidentally was exactly what I felt it was doing. Nothing could describe more accurately my state of ill-health.

Did all my selfish little heart bleed for her? Not a bit of it. I was appalled at the thought that my happiness might suddenly come to an end. And I was not so naïve as to underestimate the danger of what six months' absence could do to Robert—fiery, impetuous, bursting with health and liable to be sent by the *Morning Post* at a moment's notice to some outlandish place where he would quickly forget me. Had he not proved a dozen times with Effie that he was hard and callous?

We were having supper at the Carlton Grill, where there were never many people. Sometimes there was Sir James Barrie at his favourite table against the wall, quite alone. Little pangs of jealousy were springing up inside me. 'What happened to those two girls you met at Oxford?' I asked.

I wondered why, if they had made such a deep impression on him, he had not married one of them. In my unhappiness I was trying to pick a quarrel.

'I was coming to that,' he said. 'My adventure in Ireland undoubtedly did me a lot of good. Shortly afterwards the *Daily Express*, anxious as usual to be first with everything, began sending bundles of the late London edition by air to Paris. This was not nearly as simple as it sounds. Passenger services between London and Paris were in their infancy. Handley Page and Samuel Instone had begun with models little different from those that had been used during the last years of the 1914–18 war, piloted by ex-officers of the Royal Flying Corps, like Major Foot, a daring ace. The French also had a couple of services with converted war planes. They all used Croydon as a base, which was nothing but a large, empty field with a wooden hut near the road, and nobody ever thought of taking off unless the weather was just right. That meant that one sometimes waited an hour, two hours —all the morning—and then, if the clouds persisted, one packed up and went home. As a whole the French were a bit more daring than the English but the journey was so perilous that one never could be sure where one would land. An engine would cut out and then the pilot made for the first available field—turnips or maize or whatever, and lucky if he did not turn a somersault.

'Once or twice these rickety planes with their wood-and-canvas wings and uncertain engines actually collided in mid-air, and then the news would come in to the *Daily Express* office late at night. An air collision. Two passenger planes collide over a French village and fall in flames. No survivors. I was fortunate enough on one of these occasions to put a telephone call through to the local French mayor and get an eye-witness account of the tragedy. As there had been several British passengers on board my interview made front page news. R. D. Blumenfeld was impressed that one of his junior reporters could conduct an interview over a difficult, noisy continental line in French. He noted the fact for future use.

'So when they decided to send those bundles of late London editions over to Paris by air I was told to accompany them and write it up. There was, of course, no shortage of English language newspapers in Paris. The Continental *Daily Mail*, the *New York Herald* and the *Chicago Tribune* all had Paris editions, printed and published there, on sale at the same time as the many French national papers, of which there was a great number were: *Le Matin* and *Le Petit Parisien*, comparable to the *Daily Mail* and the *Daily Express* in England, vast circulation papers struggling for supremacy, *Le Petit Journal*, a daily newspaper entirely devoted to the theatre called *Comoedia*, beautifully produced, and *l'Auto* which specialized in the new motor car industry and the national sport of bicycle racing. But hitherto the London dailies had travelled by the Newhaven–Dieppe service and reached Paris in the afternoon, just as the Paris dailies did not arrive in the Soho shops till between 4 and 5 p.m. Thus when an aeroplane did manage to reach Paris from Croydon by breakfast time or soon after the presence of a London morning paper on the kiosks in the boulevards made a certain impact.

'Perhaps because of all this when it became necessary to appoint somebody to the Paris office, the choice fell on me.

'I found myself a most elegant room at the Hôtel du Louvre, and my windows looked all the way up the Avenue de l'Opéra to the noble façade of the Paris Opera House. There could not have been a more enchanting view in all the city. The walls of the room and the furniture in it were light green bordered with white, and the bathroom was in the same colour scheme. For this I paid twenty-eight francs a day which, because in those days the dollar and sterling were the monarchs of the world's currencies, cost me a total of barely £2 a week.

'The *Daily Express* office was in a very pretty new building at the corner of the rue de Grammont and the Boulevard des Italiens, the windows looking down on the wide tree-lined boulevard over the awning of one of those large elegant cafés which in aspect could have changed very little since the days of the Second Empire, when gentlemen rode horseback down the centre of the road and women in bonnets and crinolines sat at little tables under the trees enjoying an ice. These cafés still had a vaguely literary, theatrical or social clientele according to their history. At all events they provided one with a comfortable table, writing-paper, pen and envelopes (these three commodities under the title of "de quoi écrire"), all the morning newspapers attached to wooden rods, and soft music from a string orchestra. As they were never uncomfortably crowded one could stay there all day for the price of an apéritif, and many French authors went to their favourite café not only to meet their friends but also to write their books.

'In some ways, working in the Paris office was not so very different from working in Shoe Lane. Harry Greenwall was the Paris correspondent and he would send me out on stories much as J. B. Wilson had sent me out, hither and thither across the town in London. The fact of being bilingual to the extent of hardly knowing in which language I spoke was pleasant though it may lead as one grows older to serious complications.

'The telephone was still archaic and though we had a fixed-time call at 9 o'clock every evening at which the result of our day's work was communicated, generally by me, to London, it was practically impossible to put another call through to them without several hours' delay—which had the obvious advantage that London had such difficulties in getting through to us that we enjoyed comparative peace.

'Paris, of course, was very full, but not so that it was difficult to find accommodation in hotels, in restaurants, in theatres or on the *wagon-lits* of long-distance European trains. There always appeared to be room for everybody. One was not obliged to plan things in advance—and one decided everything on the spur of the moment, which made life very agreeable. The expensive hotels were full of Americans who came with their families and immense trunks of dresses, shoes and hats for every possible occasion, and one found them in the more famous restaurants on the boulevards, the Champs Elysées and in the Bois de Boulogne. As the women, for the most part, were gay and beautifully dressed they tended to add colour to the general scene. After dark they went to Maxim's and the Folies Bergère, while Parisians flocked to whatever restaurants were currently in vogue, where one ate in summer in the open air deliciously for very little money —leg of lamb with fresh beans and large portions from strawberry tarts over three feet long, or wood strawberries, freshly picked, with thick cream. Afterwards all the narrow little streets of Montmartre sprang alive with those tiny dance spots which the French called *boîtes* and in which people danced frenetically, going from one place to another, with paper caps on their heads, mingling with the crowds in the Place Pigalle, where roundabouts and all the fun of the fair stretched as far as the eye could see along the Boulevard de Clichy.'

For Robert the change from London where the L.C.C. had been making all that fuss over a brave little cabaret show at the Hotel Metropole in Northumberland Avenue was delightful. Though London remained the beloved capital of his childhood, Paris evoked not only the spontaneous gaiety of a land whose language he had spoken, side by side with his own, since infancy but also a more tangible proximity with the other countries of Europe—Germany, where everything was in turmoil, Switzerland with its international conferences and Italy where the rumblings of a new regime were already beginning to be felt.

'Francis de Croisset lost no time in inviting me to their home in the Place des États-Unis,' he said. 'I was curiously shy of confronting this distinguished playwright whose family I had entertained at Oxford, and who had perhaps been innocently responsible for my desire to go out more quickly into the world than if I had stayed at Magdalen to take a degree. I dressed carefully, took a taxi and rang at the door of a house that looked like a nobleman's mansion. I remember being shown into a vast room in which were Mme de Croisset, her mother, the Comtesse de Chevigné, and Marie-Laure, who introduced me to her step-father. There may have been other people in the room, I don't remember. On my arrival they all spoke English, impeccably but with what one might call a slight society drawl, but having paid me this compliment they just as naturally resumed their conversation in French. Francis de Croisset, suave, elegant, extremely handsome and with the assurance that goes with success, the most popular Paris playwright of the moment, did everything to put me at my ease. The fact that I was attached to a great London newspaper gave me an importance in his eyes which was the exact opposite of the impression that it made on Effie and on Burr. In Burr's eyes it was slightly degrading; in de Croisset's it put me (quite unjustifiably) on a par with all the writers in Paris who, besides being novelists, playwrights or historians, were fundamentally journalists. Incidentally so were politicians from the Premier down. They all wrote for the papers and proudly signed their articles. Some weeks before I had left London,

Francis de Croisset had sent me a letter telling me that he had an important conference the following week for which he needed certain details that I could more easily obtain for him in London. Would I cable? Having discovered the information he needed I compressed it into 500 words and filed it by cable that same night. This was the sort of usefulness that would make of me an ally. In return, he said, I would discover that his friends in Paris would become mine. He would introduce me to whomsoever I pleased.

'But how ignorant I was! Who had warned me that the aristocratic little woman keeping up a stream of witty comments as she sat very upright in her armchair, this dynamic grandmother, Mme de Chevigné, then—as I now know—sixty-three years old, was the model for Marcel Proust's Mme de Guermantes! No wonder that Marie-Laure after our happy hours gliding in a punt down the Cherwell under the red and white hawthorn, had sent me *A l'ombre des Jeunes Filles en Fleurs*, winner of the Prix Goncourt the previous year (1919), and *Du côté de Guermantes* (1920) inscribed and hot off the presses.

'In company she prided herself on being descended from the Marquis de Sade and her conversation, whether purposely or not, was spiced. Marie-Laure incidentally, for this same reason had been called Laure, after Laure de Noves, the wife of Hugues de Sade who was immortalized by Petrarch.

'Momentarily, because I was so naïve and shy, Mme de Chevigné shocked me, first because she began making a great to-do about the shoes that her grand-daughter, Laure, was wearing. How much had she paid for them? So little money? She had guessed as much. Had she paid more money for her shoes, they would have been more elegant. Nobody ever gets anything for nothing—even shoes! And from this subject she turned quickly to another—to the engagement of a young girl who must have been Marie-Laure's contemporary, a wealthy French girl. Mme de Chevigné clearly disapproved of the young man she was in love with. "But why?" asked her daughter, Mme de Croisset. "Because," answered her mother with a wicked smile, "anybody can see that il n'a rien derrière la brayette!—that he has nothing behind his trouser flies!"'

Was Robert, in telling me this story, trying to shock me as he claimed to have been shocked himself? What was I to make of his gradual introduction into a world so different from that of his contemplative parents at Brentford? The Paris he talked about, that Paris of 1922, had very little in common with the Paris I had left as a girl of fifteen in 1921. This only served to show the immense gulf that divided us until we met and our interests fused.

Robert spent all that summer—the summer of 1922—as assistant Paris correspondent of the *Daily Express*. His hotel, which became a home to him, was next to the Théâtre Français, and this allowed him to become familiar with the plays of Molière and Racine, of Beaumarchais and Alfred de Musset. The book-shop opposite, one of the largest in Paris, was the rendezvous of such writers as Porto-Riche and Anatole France, who could often be seen browsing amongst the yellow-back volumes or talking with other writers who came to see how their books were selling. Then also there was the Café de la Régence with its marble-topped tables and its string orchestra, where actors and actresses of the Com-édie Française came after the final curtain to discuss their affairs.

There was the narrow, picturesque rue Sainte Anne along which Robert walked several times a day on his way to and from the office in the rue de Grammont. Here many small traders continued as craftsmen, furniture dealers making their tables and chairs on the pavement as in the eighteenth century, women ironing damp linen or making infinitesimal pleats in crêpe de chine lingerie with a flick of the wrist, and an artistry which has utterly disappeared.

Then in August things happened which were greatly to affect his future.

Eighteen months earlier—in March 1921—just about the time he had walked out of that Divinity paper exam. at Oxford, the Greeks, feeling very proud of themselves because, by the Treaty of Sèvres the previous August, they had been awarded practically all Thrace outside Constantinople, and a mandate over Smyrna, launched an attack in Asia Minor. For a time it went well, but as soon as winter set in, Kemal took advantage of the bad weather to reorganize the Turkish army, and he was now in the middle of such a violent offensive that the Greeks were on the run.

This would not have worried Robert very much except that the London office mentioned over the telephone that Lord Beaverbrook had gone to Deauville and that it would be wise to keep an eye on that fashionable resort, which at this time of year was always apt, with its horse-racing and high gambling at the casino, its polo, elegant women and millionaires, to burst into the news. In fact, Lord Beaverbrook, besides amusing himself, took advantage of his visit to meet his friend the Aga Khan who, like Sem, the cartoonist, Mlle Chanel and many others never missed a Deauville season. The Aga Khan, as leading spokesman of the Moslem world, was worried because of Lloyd George's antagonism towards Turkey, and he wondered if Lord Beaverbrook could not help reconcile the British and Turkish points of view. He even suggested that if Lord Beaverbrook were willing to go to Turkey, he would arrange for him to meet important people there. On Lord Beaverbrook's return to England he invited Lloyd George, Winston Churchill and Lord Birkenhead to his country house at Cherkley near Leatherhead in Surrey but he made little headway. Accordingly Lord Beaverbrook decided to take the Aga Khan's advice and set off towards the end of the month for Constantinople.

But by the beginning of September the Turks had reached Smyrna and had driven the Greeks into the sea. Not since the fall of Sevastopol had there been anything quite like this—so much bloodshed, so many, many people slain under a sky reddened by the flames of buildings on fire. The sea was full of floating corpses that routed soldiers fished out of the water so as to go through their pockets in the hope of finding money or valuables. Smyrna, the pearl of the Aegean, the Queen of the Orient, the Turkish part of the town against high hills crowned by Byzantine ramparts now reduced to ruins against the hot sky; the Armenian population so determined to die rather than to suffer Turkish domination that it had set fire to their own homes; the English colony having made a last-minute escape in the Greek steamer *Elpiniki* for London. British, French and Italian warships were watching from a distance outside the harbour. What would Britain do?

At this point, Robert received instructions from London to go to interview the Aga Khan in Deauville. What about? Nobody had thought to tell him but it was probably Lord Beaverbrook's way of reassuring the Aga Khan about the anxiety he had shown over British policy in that part of the world. Deauville, deserted except for the Aga Khan at the Normandy Hotel and Venizelos, who had also prolonged his holiday there, was empty and at its loveliest. Deauville in August is merely a crowded plage. In September the creeper over the Normandy Hotel turns red and all the orchards are full of cider apples. Robert, getting out of the Paris train, fell madly in love with this empty Deauville and made a vow that he would one day buy a home in this part of the world. That is why, though I could not guess it at this moment, when I was a very hesitating bride, this Normandy coast was to play so important a role in my future life.

On his way back to England, Lord Beaverbrook stopped at Athens, and sent a report to his paper describing the routed Greek army's return to Piraeus. Three army officers, amongst them a certain Colonel Plastiras, staged a revolution of sorts in Athens, overthrew King Constantine in favour of his son George, and sent a telegram to Venizelos. Venizelos, who had brought the Greeks into the 1914–18 war on the side of the Allies, was living in France since he had been defeated in the last elections. In fact he was still in Deauville but on receipt of the telegram went to London to see Lloyd George and then back to Paris to talk to M. Poincaré.

Robert, meanwhile, was back at the Hôtel du Louvre, where he vaguely took note of Mussolini's rise to power in Italy and the march on Rome; and glanced at pictures of Lord Carnavon and Mr Howard Carter, candles in hand, opening the tomb of Tutankhamen in the Valley of the Kings. He had no reason to suppose that he was suddenly going to cross Europe.

In England the Cabinet had decided to hold a General Election on a Coalition ticket. In Beaverbrook's opinion Lloyd George's Greek policy had harmed his prestige, and Bonar Law was the obvious choice for the Conservative leadership. Things worked out as he predicted. Lloyd George resigned and Bonar Law, after first securing election as leader of the Conservative Party, became Prime Minister.

In November, Robert received a cable telling him to go immediately to Lausanne, where a conference had begun to try to settle the war between the Turks and the defeated Greeks. Something had happened to the correspondent who was supposed to be covering it. Robert, expecting only to be there for a couple of days, did not trouble even to go back to his hotel for a bag. On the morning when he took a cab from the station to the Hôtel Beaurivage, snow lay all over the city and the air was deliciously cold and invigorating. Lord Curzon and the English delegation were already at the hotel; at the Lausanne Palace in the centre of the town were the French, the Turkish, the Japanese and the Egyptians, their national flags floating over the entrance. But the imagination of the public was centred on Mussolini, the hero of the March on Rome (though, in fact, he had not taken part in it, arriving in Rome the following morning by train), and Tchitcherine, the Bolshevist who in his red waistcoat and with his pointed beard turned up at the tip looked rather like a figure in a comic opera who, to please the press, allowed himself to be photographed in his hotel suite wearing the uniform of a general in the Red Army. Mussolini proved such an attraction that women peered through keyholes to look at him. He was aware of it, and could be seen passing through the foyer carefully turned out with a stiff, winged collar, striped tie, diamond tie-pin, white spats and a top hat. He liked to be noticed in the company of Lord Curzon, stern and proud, gripping the lapels of his morning coat, and with Poincaré, in a lounge suit and gloves.

Robert was enjoying the deep snow and pure crisp air of Lausanne with its wide streets and beautiful shops when he was told to catch the Simplon–Orient Express for Athens. He could hardly believe it. In all Europe there was no more romantic journey. Was he really going to see the violet hills of Greece and the purple sea of Homer's Odyssey? To what did he owe such immense good fortune?

Five of King Constantine's former ministers, brought before a revolutionary court-martial in Athens, in spite of repeated pleas for mercy by the British Government, had been condemned to death for incompetence in the war against Turkey—and within only a few hours of the verdict, taken to a place outside Athens called Goudi and shot. Murdered—the English newspapers had called it.

Why did Britain react so violently? The unfortunate ministers had not only been incompetent but they had served a king who had just been banished for the second time for being pro-German. Was he not the ex-Kaiser's brother-in-law? Had it not been for Venizelos, Greece would never have come in on the Allied side during the 1914–18 war.

But Colonel Plastiras, responsible for the shootings, was the new strong man of Greece, and after the defeat of the army had proudly entered Athens riding a charger—and the Allies were probably suspicious of military dictators, even if they were on the right side of the fence.

Traversing Europe in his *wagon-lit*, Robert looked out with eyes full of wonder—Venice, so beloved by Peli, Zagreb, Belgrade, Sofia, Salonica in ruins, and then past Mount Olympus to Larissa—slowly, slowly, down on the way to Athens. Oh, those Greek hills and olive trees so evocative of the past with hardly ever a living person to destroy the illusion of having stepped back into classical times. Callous in so many ways, he wept.

Athens had not changed, as far as one could tell, in a hundred years. War had allowed its low, white buildings to look shabby but no foreign trippers walked its dusty streets. The Parthenon rose in all its glory over sweet-smelling hills and distant sea, and oranges had begun to ripen in the garden of the royal palace where Constantine's son, King George, was virtually a prisoner. Evzones, with their pointed shoes and white skirts, kept guard outside the offices of Colonel Plastiras. Old men at street corners warmed Turkish coffee in copper pots. In cafés, Greeks bought lottery tickets for a scraggy chicken.

Tragedy, no less real than the loss of a battle, hung over the beautiful city. Cholera and typhus were rife. A ship filled with refugees from the Black Sea had been one of many cruising in Greek waters trying to get permission to enter harbour. Nobody would receive it. Robert first saw it through a group of olive trees riding at anchor on a stretch of sheltered water. The yellow flag hung limply from its mast. A young New York doctor in charge of the vessel had set out from Samsun in the Black Sea with 2,000 refugees. Cholera, typhus and smallpox broke out in turn. There remained only 400 passengers not stricken, and owing to the danger of infection, the bodies of the victims were burnt in the ship's furnace. In Athens, 1,000 refugees were dying every day. Crowds flocked to the cathedrals of Holy Trinity and Siridion but in each place of worship a member of the congregation sank to the floor, and the people flocked out in panic, leaving only the priests at the altar.

As Christmas approached the story of the murdered ministers was forgotten, the plague subsided and the oranges in King George's palace garden became more golden. A very different ship was now steaming towards Phaleron Bay. The *Mauretania*, the most popular of all the Cunard transatlantic liners, was making a cruise in the Mediterranean for millionaires—and Lord Beaverbrook was on board with a small party of friends. How lovely this beautiful ship looked in the moonlight with its gleaming white superstructure and red funnels!

A white dusty road, right against the water's edge, followed the sweeping curve of the bay as one drove from the Parthenon to Piraeus. Here one stood waiting for a motor launch to take one to the anchored ship. It was Robert's first meeting with Lord Beaverbrook. On the shore, the owner of the *Daily Express* stood a moment distributing drachmas to a crowd of Greek children who had come to look at this peaceful invasion from another world.

Then in a rather battered car, one of the only taxis in Athens, Robert and Lord Beaverbrook drove up to the Parthenon and into the city.

How full of possibilities this short journey between the little shops and low white buildings! How picturesque with the orange trees and the little Greek boys offering salted crescents of bread strung on a stick, the country farmers selling eggs and chickens, the vendors of coloured silk carrying out their wares. I sometimes wondered how Robert would have used these few moments if he could have lived them over again.

But the next day, together with James Douglas, a staff writer on the *Sunday Express*, they took a hamper from the *Mauretania* and drove to the Delphic Oracle, where they lay on the thyme-scented rocks under the midday sun while James Douglas, who was always moralizing about something, read out information from a guide-book till suddenly silenced by Lord Beaverbrook, wise enough to prefer the silence of the surrounding hills. Here was no living thing but the birds overhead.

Consider for a moment what the Oracle could have told his lordship as he lay with his clasped hands behind his head, his hat tipped forward on his impish features. Perhaps that within a few months Lord Beaverbrook's best friend, Bonar Law, 'the best government this generation has seen', would be found to have incurable cancer of the throat, and that in less than a year he would be dead.

7

AFTER A WONDERFUL CHRISTMAS evening which we had spent dancing together at the Berkeley Hotel, Robert took everything in hand. He watched over me as I had dreamt of watching over him, and gave orders not only to me but to my mother. I was to leave the Savoy immediately, and my mother and I were to spend the rest of the winter in the Pyrenees. When I was well again, Robert and I would be married. It all sounded very simple.

My absence lasted much longer than we had foreseen, and my mother was obliged to come home first, leaving me behind to complete my cure. As I have told all this in *Madeleine Grown Up*, I do not need to go over it again. Robert took me to Brentford to say goodbye to his parents, and then drove us to Victoria station to catch the Paris boat-express.

I still remember Pau as a beautiful city—but, oh, the funerals that passed under our hotel window! Most of our fellow guests in the hotel were living in slow motion, either ill or convalescing from pleurisy, pneumonia or anaemia.

On the other side of the Pyrenees, lay Spain. Oh, how I dreamt of it and of finding myself amongst young people living normal lives. I bought a bottle of Chanel's Gardenia perfume, and wore it constantly, so that today if ever I smell it on somebody, I recall the terrible anxieties of my youth, and how I despaired of ever getting well again. There was an old gentleman who played cards every evening in the hotel lounge. Most of the guests spent their far too long evenings doing precisely this. He once said to me that though life was a precarious business, he was always surprised by the resistance of the human body. When he was alone he would sit for hours with a pack of cards trying to succeed with what was known as the Marie-Antoinette patience, this

unhappy queen having tried it unsuccessfully during the terrible
days preceding her execution by the guillotine, so it was said.
Sometimes he would succeed where she had failed, and then his
mood would change from despair to hope. But all this was not a
particularly helpful atmosphere for my state of mind.

Shortly before Easter my mother thought it wise to renew
contact with her customers in London. She was not even now at
all sure that my marriage would take place, and she had said:
'If Robert gets tired of waiting, and after all, one could not
blame him. ... He's young and ambitious. ... Now, don't cry.
These things are better said than written. It sounds cruel, but so
much of what happens to me is cruel. We were much happier in
our poverty, sewing by the lamp. ... You can go on believing in
him, if you want to, but it's my duty, being older and more
experienced, to warn you against a possible disappointment.'

She was in the armchair, crying softly. Her skin seemed grey
and she looked suddenly old.

It was late autumn when I finally returned to London, rested,
happier, more confident, my eyes bright with a rediscovered
desire for life. Effie had written me long, affectionate letters;
others less tender from my mother, scarcely hid her continued
anxiety. The long boat-train drew up at the continental arrival
platform at Victoria station. Robert was waiting for me, slim,
smiling, his blue eyes full of tender love. How marvellous it all
seemed. We fell into one another's arms and then I looked round
for Matilda. She was not there. Well, never mind. At least, I had
Robert.

When later I went round to Stacey Street, my mother said:

'Lucille [introduced in *Madeleine Grown Up*] dropped in, and
so as it was Saturday we thought we'd both go to fetch you at the
station. We walked to Victoria, or at least we walked half way but
we suddenly jumped on a bus, fearing to be late, and then, I'm not
quite sure how, we arrived an hour before the train was due. So
we both waited patiently. When the train came in I was in such a
state that I couldn't see anything. Lucille cried out:

'Oh, look! Madeleine is wearing a pink hat! If only you knew
how pretty she is!'

'I looked and I saw the hat, but as Robert was there, kissing you, I sighed, and I said to Lucille: 'Everything is all right now. They are happy. Let's go!'

Because Robert had taken an apartment in Conduit Street, the wedding took place one Saturday morning at St George's, Hanover Square, and as at the wedding of Hannah de Rothschild and Henry FitzRoy, everybody felt a bit guilty. Effie arrived by bus and tube, having left the vicar, her dearest Burr, at home, he having refused, poor, hurt soul, to marry us in his own church at Brentford.

Robert and I stayed on for a little while in the small furnished apartment he had taken over the then very fashionable Ambassador's Club in Conduit street, half way between Bond Street and Hanover Square. But from the beginning he had only intended it to be a temporary arrangement to tide over that difficult period immediately preceding our wedding, so that we could meet more easily on common ground. Now that I was married, my visits to Matilda in Stacey Street took on an absurdly formal air, and I would sit rather self-consciously and very straight-backed on the edge of the couch under the window that had formerly been my bed, just like all the other women who came to visit my mother to order a dress or to gossip for half an hour. These visits tore at my heart. Robert was earning no more at the *Morning Post* than when eight years earlier he had first gone to the *Daily Express*, and there was very little left of the nest-egg that Effie had given him on his twenty-first birthday and which had allowed us to have such lovely evenings in quiet restaurants during the difficult period of our engagement. He spoilt me terribly but I had no personal allowance which I could have used to better my mother's financial position. He bought me the love-liest clothes from the Galeries Lafayette in Regent Street, where I had once worked as a junior salesgirl, and most of my acces-sories—bags, shoes and hats—came from Paris. Roberts and Carroll, a famous women's tailor in Cork Street, who made riding-habits for those aristocratic women who hunted with the Prince of Wales, made me a black coat and skirt for my wedding, and later a blue one, neither deep blue nor royal blue but the colour of cornflowers when they are still in bud and about to open. With this I wore a real lace blouse, almost a museum piece, that my mother had made me from her small store of hand-made lace, and against which my Florentine brooch of gold and pearls looked truly lovely. But when I arrived thus dressed with beautiful fox furs and a beige hat to visit my mother in her one-room apartment, something was obviously wrong.

In fact, all of us in this complicated story were about to suffer a great change. To begin with, Robert and I needed a home. We were both determined to live in the heart of the town, chiefly because we loved it and would have been unhappy anywhere but within a 2*d.* bus ride from Piccadilly Circus. As there had not yet been a building boom after the 1914–18 war modern apartments were difficult to find and extremely expensive. We chose one on the third floor of a building just completed at the corner of Brompton Road and Beauchamp Place but it had no heating of any kind and the walls were still damp. Water for the kitchen and the bath came from a geyser, and built-in cupboards and wardrobes were still things of the future.

For a bride looking forward to a home of her own, I was not spoilt, for neither of us owned any furniture and after having carpets to put down on the bare floor-boards, we would doubtless have been obliged to camp in this cold and uninviting home if Effie had not taken me to Harrods to buy me a bed, an armchair and the more necessary additional pieces of furniture. But there were compensations. Robert who had been unhappy on the *Morning Post* was sent on a four days' cruise on a new Cunarder, so that the great shipping company could show this wonderful vessel to the press. The newspaper world was always given a wonderful time on occasions like this one. Nothing was ever too good for them. No collection of millionaires could have been treated more royally. During this trip Robert became friendly with Victor Suhr, a very experienced journalist who was news editor of the London *Evening News,* and no sooner were they back in London than Mr FitzHugh, the editor, invited Robert to Carmelite House where, on Victor Suhr's instigation, he was offered what was to prove the happiest job of his newspaper career.

So we not only had a home (however bare) but Robert had a wonderful job.

Wonderful also for me was this hitherto unknown part of London, the fashionable end in which one met shopping at Harrods all that were left of titled English Society gravitating round the pleasure-seeking Prince of Wales and Prince George, in a final, colourful flutter, like gay and beautiful butterflies about to have their wings burnt in the coming collapse of an era. Their world would last, as Marie-Antoinette's had done, for just a few short years, but at least I would have seen it, as Effie, in spite of her repugnance to it, had seen the end of an era in which Peli played so important a role from the house in Hans Place, just behind Harrods, in which she had entertained all the greatest painters, writers, musicians and poets of the second half of the Victorian age. It was curious how in so many small ways I was beginning to tread in her shoes.

How delightfully I found myself slipping into the life of a young married woman. As soon as Robert left in the morning, I could turn over in the cool linen sheets of our big double bed and go off to sleep again. No longer need I fear wet mornings (which meant wet shoes and mud-splashed silk stockings) and the racing minute-hand of the alarm clock. To do what I pleased, when I pleased—except that I was limited in money, though to economize was merely a question of discipline. We had always economized. But to be free! Not to have Matilda always just behind my shoulder to criticize. This is what marriage had brought me. To take lots of time to choose a dress, to play with the cat, to do my hair and to make up my face. All this was heaven. I put on my pink hat and in no time at all, in less than three minutes, I am at Harrods! I bought practically everything at Harrods, as did Peli, as did Effie. I even bought my bread there, the steak for lunch, the fruit and vegetables. I was a thousand times happier doing this than if I had been taken to Venice for a honeymoon. Harrods was my fairy-tale come true. My Aladdin's cave. Robert was earning more money on the *Evening News* and occasionally had a bonus. I bought coloured linen sheets, double sheets of the very best Irish linen—pink, blue or green—and pillow-cases to match for fifty shillings a pair, even cheaper at the sales, and Effie, because at heart she was extraordinarily feminine, had the delightful idea of sending me a cheque for £25 for the white sales. She loved counting her sheets in the linen cupboard at Brentford, putting lavender sachets amongst them, and so she sympathized with me.

The apartment was still half empty but Effie had sent me all Robert's books, which filled three tea-chests, and I had emptied them out into one of the rooms, waiting to order bookshelves. Included amongst them were those that Marie-Laure had sent him from Paris, the first, inscribed editions of those novels by Marcel Proust, and all the plays of Francis de Croisset; hundreds of books in French, in English, as well as the classics, both in Greek and Latin and in translations. These were to be my university, my apprenticeship to our joint life on the *Evening News*.

You might think that it had been necessary for me to rush out to buy crockery. But as in everything else, we never did the accepted thing. Effie arrived one morning with a tea-set that had once been Peli's at Hans Place. A few cups and saucers were missing. It had red roses painted on what is known as egg-china, so delicate that one could see through the cups and saucers. The roses were of such a deep hue that I have never since seen anything like them. They were probably Viennese, but when much later I tried to match them up in the famous shop near the Hofburg, they told me that the set must have been made more than a century earlier and that the secret was lost. Since then all the pieces but the milk jug have been broken, and this I keep for flowers. Effie also brought me a great quantity of china with blue flowers which Peli more ordinarily used at Hans Place and which design she never altered, so that when anything was broken it could be replaced without anybody noticing.

My mother-in-law had come up to town on what she called a routine expedition. She asked me if I would like to come shopping with her—and, of course, I exclaimed in delight. Nothing could have amused me more. She was not strong enough to do much walking, and though we never went much beyond Sloane Street we took taxis everywhere. She was anxious to buy knitting wool and a cashmere dressing-gown for Burr. 'Afterwards, we shall come back to *your* place, and you shall make me a cup of real French coffee.' To *my* place! What a sweet sound in my ears.

It was while drinking real French coffee (from a percolator) at my place, that she began talking to me again about Peli. But I noticed, as indeed I had noticed from the first, that she seldom, if ever, spoke of her father, Sir Coutts Lindsay. Effie now reminded me that Hannah, having so recently lost both her little boy, Arthur, and her beloved husband, Henry FitzRoy, then Minister of Works responsible for Big Ben, had been herself near to death when her daughter Blanche, having blossomed out into a beautiful young woman, had fallen in love with Sir Coutts. Nobody dared tell Blanche that Sir Coutts already had a mistress, an artist's model, to whom he was still greatly attached. Or if they did tell her, she was too headstrong to listen. For how long did the marriage remain a happy one? Like all the marriages in Effie's family, it had been celebrated in unusual circumstances. Hannah's health was so precarious that the wedding was to take place by special licence in the bride's home in Upper Grosvenor Street. On the last day of June, while a hot sun streamed into the drawing-room, Blanche, in a white dress, was married by the Canon of Westminster, the Rev. Evan Nepean, to the man she loved. In the room above, Hannah, too ill to come down, had opened the Prayer Book that her husband had given her when they were married, and her lips moved slightly as she followed the service. She desired but one thing, that this marriage should be a long and happy one. She would not live to know.

How long, in fact, did Blanche remain happily married?

For at least a few brilliant years after the opening of the Grosvenor Gallery. Her name had become synonymous with the Pre-Raphaelite movement which, though first conceived in the forties by William Holman Hunt and Dante Gabriel Rossetti, who shared a studio in Cleveland Street, and John Everett Millais, was to soar into fame under her guidance. These three, together with Watts, Whistler, and Edward Burne-Jones, gathered round her. G. F. Watt's finest portrait is of Blanche Lindsay playing her violin, a portrait which I was eventually to own. John Millais was a constant visitor and friend. One day after tea Blanche showed him up to the nursery where four-year-old Effie was with her nurse, Mrs Baillie. My future mother-in-law, a fair-haired little girl in a white frock, was kneeling at the feet of her aged nurse, who wore a lace cap on her head and was reading to her from a picture book. Thus he came to paint the picture which I had seen hanging in Robert's room at Brentford. Unfortunately it was stolen from my farm in Normandy during the German occupation in the Second World War. The Lindsays would also spend happy months back at Balcarres, the gardens of which were laid out at immense expense by Blanche. Prince Leopold, Queen Victoria's youngest son, would often invite himself for a week's holiday there. But even after the parting, Blanche did not abandon her artistic career—perhaps she even widened it. She wrote:

'Burne-Jones and his wife were very kind to me when my marriage turned definitely unhappy. They allowed me to go and paint early in the morning at The Grange in a studio next to the one in which he worked, and afterwards to stay to luncheon. In those days their daughter was still unmarried. I remember her vividly, particularly in the garden one summer afternoon. She sat swinging herself on the low branches of an apple tree, the blossoms all above and around her. She was dressed in a cotton gown of that blue that her father liked so much, and she wore a big straw hat. I thought her one of the most beauteous things I had ever seen, with her wonderful eyes and exquisite oval face. Then on Sunday I was invited to supper, a simple and informal meal. No late hours were kept. Sometimes a bottle of some wonderful Cyprus wine was opened and Burne-Jones would exclaim: "It is just what must have been drunk by Aphrodite, goddess of love, when she rose from the sea!" One day when he was painting, he said laughingly: "I never could show anyone how to paint. Now, watch carefully how I do this. If you were not looking, I should certainly do it in quite a different way."

'Burne-Jones and the poet William Morris breakfasted together every Sunday morning. They never gave this habit up, even in illness, till the hand of death parted the poet and teller of sagas from the painter who was so much at one with him in thought.'

I am today surrounded by paintings of Blanche Lindsay at various times of her life. There is one that Effie did not care for. It shows her as a young wife seated on a red couch in a bow window at

Balcarres. She wears a black velvet bandeau in her hair and a grey flounced dress with white lace on the collar and cuffs, and a blue brooch. There is a yellow cockatoo preening itself on her lap and her violin lies within reach of her hand on the couch. What is particular about this portrait is that it shows her looking out of the window with a rather sad expression on her youthful features as if seeking something beyond the green foliage running up the side of the house. Helen, Effie's sister, who was at Balcarres at the time told me that Sir Coutts had a young woman guest with whom Blanche believed he was in love in the room while he was painting the picture. Blanche, unwilling to look upon her, had chosen to turn her head so that she could gaze sorrowfully out of the window.

Though Robert had joined the *Evening News* as a reporter, which after all when one is young is the thing to be on a newspaper, he became suddenly something else. The paper had a very important diary on its leader page which often ran to two full columns, and was at that time written as a more or less consecutive narrative describing what the writer had done in town on the previous day. This technique, later considered old-fashioned, was to give whoever wrote it almost limitless scope. One described lunch with this person, tea with that one, a flower show in the country, a first night at a London theatre, supper at such or such a restaurant with a glimpse perhaps of the Prince of Wales dancing a blues or a tango, a walk back home through the Park at 2 a.m. and if the daffodils were beginning to bloom on the way to the office the next morning. Probably no other job in all Fleet Street could have given Robert and myself such an interesting time. While he looked after the more serious sides, I would provide the feminine touches. What had the lucky girl who danced cheek-to-cheek with the Prince of Wales or Prince George worn at Quaglino's or at the Savoy last night?

We continued to go to Brentford almost every Saturday afternoon. Robert had bought what was then known as a clover-leaf Citroën second-hand for £20. As it used up hardly any petrol and never went wrong, and was so small and light that one could leave it about without too often incurring the wrath of the police, we became very attached to it. Motor cars had not yet cluttered up the town and were never left unoccupied at the side of the street.

Effie was beginning to mention the possibility of retirement, though with considerable sadness in her voice because Brentford and her parishioners were all her life and she could not imagine herself away from them. But Burr was on the eve of his seventieth birthday, and the Ecclesiastical Commissioners were being offered immense sums for this green oasis, this little patch of Paradise that so insolently belonged to the Church between giant breweries and expanding gas works. What right had the king-fisher to make his nest at the bottom of the osier eyot or the mulberry tree, planted in the reign of Charles the First, to drop its luscious black fruit on a vicarage lawn? Did people still go to church?

The vicar's birthday was on 2nd August. What could one give to a man who had such modest needs? He had found in Effie perfect love. His affection for her was so touching that I could never feel angry with him for having refused to marry Robert and me in his church. He had never done a wrong thing in his life. Generally, faced with the problem of buying him a birthday gift, we looked for some amusing thing, some cheap little toy that would make him laugh. For, as I have already said, he had this almost childish side, this ability to look upon life through the eyes of a boy. We would also try to find something for his dog, his pekinese, on the grounds that what gave pleasure to the dog would give pleasure to him also.

While Robert and Effie were in the dining-room, I went off to find Burr in his study. I would spend ten minutes alone with him on his seventieth birthday. I would do my very best to make him give me one of those amused smiles that would occasionally light up his large, homely features—his ecclesiastical features, because one could never imagine his being anything else but a clergyman.

I found him in his favourite position seated behind his enor-mous roll-top desk, one leg raised and reposing on a pulled-out top drawer at the side. He loved to have one leg out and supported in this way. I never understood why, but long afterwards I caught Robert doing the same thing and chided him for it. Burr's desk was an amazing clutter of shelves and pigeon-holes stuffed with papers that he had not looked at for five or ten years but which he considered too precious to throw away. Dressed as always in a shiny, threadbare black parson's suit, with his hard white parson's collar, he beamed at me a friendly welcome. I think that what he had really lacked at the time of our wedding was enough time to get to know me. He was one of those men who need to see you about the place for five or ten years before it strikes them to say good-morning. Now, at last—but almost too late—I had become automatically part of the family. His beaming features were proof of it, though he said nothing.

I broached all sorts of subjects—the heat of this torrid August day, the flowers in the garden, the fruit on the trees, an astute compliment to what the Conservatives were doing in the country, and had he made any money on the Stock Exchange? He owned £1,000 of his own, a life's savings, put away in little yearly sums from his stipend of £400 a year, and he invested it in tiny packets of £100 or less in all sorts of different British companies on the Stock Exchange, chosen not because he had any inside knowledge about them but because they were English—English to the core. He had a lot of fun looking at the evening paper—the *Evening News*—at tea-time to see whether any of them had gone up by 3*d.* or a shilling.

But on this, his seventieth birthday, none of these subjects appeared to interest him, and he said suddenly:

'My mother, who was a very wonderful person, died at the age of ninety-two. In my family we all live to be very old. I hope to do the same.'

He got up slowly, and taking my arms, gently led me to the other side of the room, where a large framed photograph showed his mother in a lace cap and a tight-fitting black dress seated against the garden wall and surrounded by Effie, the children and himself.

'You are very like her,' I said, truthfully.

'Do you think so?' he asked, genuinely pleased.

Then the study door opened and Robert came in. The magical moment had passed.

We stayed to a frugal supper, some sort of fish, if I remember rightly, probably turbot, and tinned California pears, and the inevitable cut-glass jug of filtered water. I looked for some slight continuation of Burr's conversation about his mother. She had lived towards the end of her life at Southport and I hoped he might tell us about her little house and her manner of spending her birthdays, but I could get nothing out of him. The oppressive heat appeared to weigh on him and several times he alarmed us by breaking into hiccups. Perhaps he had eaten too quickly.

The weather was so menacing that I persuaded Robert to start for home rather earlier than we had originally planned. We used to put the car in a cul-de-sac off the Ealing road, where it was invariably surrounded by children but relatively safe from the eyes of prowling policemen, who would not yet tolerate a parked car anywhere near traffic. As it was virtually an open car with only a light hood that gave no protection from the sides, I was not anxious to be out in the middle of what promised soon to be a tremendous August thunderstorm.

After we had said goodnight to Effie and Burr we accordingly ran up the slope towards the High Street, which smelt more than ever of hot, dry air, gas and hops. A few moments later we had turned the car and were driving past St George's church.

'I hope you weren't too bored?' said Robert.

'On the contrary.' I said. 'In his study before supper your father started talking about his mother, and the fact that she had lived to the age of ninety-two without the loss of any of her faculties. I hoped it might be a sign that he is beginning to love me a little. After all, we are making headway. He even allows me to kiss his forehead before leaving the house. And Effie always smiles approvingly when she sees me going to him. Before supper she took me aside and told me that she had prayed so very hard that the family might keep together. The family, she said, must learn to surmount obstacles—disappointments, quarrels, anger, even if it was kept under control—and the differences that always exist between one generation and another. "Keep to-gether always," she said to me, "to the end of your lives!" I paused, there being large crowds outside the Chiswick Empire, where people were queuing up for the third house, and Robert was trying to thread his way between a band of drunks and a tramcar. 'I take it,' I said, as soon as he had safely extricated us from this danger, 'that Effie was referring to us.'

'Yes,' he agreed, 'she probably was.'

We got back just before the rain—in time to put the car away in the tiny garage mews off Montpelier Street, and open the roof door so that Pépé our black cat could come in for his supper. This was the first thing we did after looking to see if there were any letters by the 9 p.m. post and going up in the lift. The mails were so good that if my mother-in-law wrote to me in the morning I would be sure to get her letter the same evening.

Though our apartment was still inadequately furnished and extremely noisy it had, apart from its charming location, an advantage for Pépé. As our building, being modern, was taller by two storeys than all the little Victorian or Georgian houses in Beauchamp Place, a door at the end of the long corridor into which the rooms opened led out onto a small roof garden, and from there Pépé could go romping between red chimney-stacks and attic windows to the very end of the street, which was quite a long one. As on hot evenings like this one the people who lived over the shops in Beauchamp Place kept their attic windows open, Pépé would call in on them, invited or not, and accordingly had a huge circle of friends. Occasionally he would drag back in his mouth a piece of material from the little tailor up the street, and play with it as if it were a mouse. In spite of all this, he was very obedient. At whatever hour we got home at night, even if it was in the small hours of the morning after a late supper at the Embassy or the Savoy, as soon as we opened the door and called him, we would see in the moonlight his lithe black body leaping and jumping over the slates on his way back. He was, of course, a real Londoner, having being discovered as a kitten in Conduit Street by the porter of the Ambassador's Club and brought to me because I was terrified of mice.

As soon as the rain started it came down in torrents and the thunder was like gunfire, but by morning everything was calm again, and only the raindrops on the leaves of the plane trees, which shimmered in another heat haze in the street below, told of the violence of the storm.

At about midday we received a call from one of the maids at

Brentford with a message from Effie to say that during the night Burr had suffered a serious stroke and was in bed with one side of his body completely paralysed.

We were now to see poor Effie, generally so calm and full of quiet confidence, momentarily felled by despair. She even felt herself responsible for the calamity which had so swiftly and unexpectedly overtaken her dear Burr. Shortly before 10 o'clock the previous night, as they were going to bed, the pekinese, indisposed by the heat, was violently sick in the middle of a Persian carpet, and Effie, exasperated by this unhappy incident, exclaimed angrily against the animal while trying to clean up the mess. Burr himself, upset to hear her speaking roughly to his pekinese, arrived hurriedly on the scene in his dressing-gown, fearful lest Effie, in her annoyance, should put the little beast out in the garden in the middle of the storm. Great claps of thunder were shaking the house and the lightning was so vivid that it lit up the dining-room where the oil-lamp had already been extinguished.

The vicar was terrified of lightning, having in his youth seen a man who had sheltered under a tree during a storm electrocuted. Though that was the sort of thing that one read about in books when Robert and I were children, the arrival of electric light in great cities, and the diminishing loneliness of people in rural areas, had to a great extent effaced the danger from most people's minds. But Burr had put up the most complicated lightning conductors beyond the mulberry tree in his garden and something in his mind associated storms and the sound of thunder with personal disaster. Alas, his premonition was not entirely unfounded.

But while Effie blamed herself for that moment of anger, so unlike her, and in such contradiction to the words she had said to her son only a few hours earlier about not allowing anything to disunite the family, Robert himself, seeing his father inert in the white linen nightshirt in the big double bed, unable to utter a word, and paralysed all down one side, had uncomfortable thoughts of his own. Perhaps it was not so much Effie and the dog that had brought on this virtual end to his father's long life, but Robert's own action in doing almost everything he possibly could have done to disappoint him—Oxford, his career—our marriage.

I next remember seeing Burr shuffling very uncertainly across a room in a long dressing-gown and slippers, being supported by Effie. He no longer wore the clergyman's white collar, and his expression had become pathetic and guileless. He even attempted a large welcoming smile when he saw me but it was less to excuse any grudge that he might once have had against me than the fact that he had now fallen into this state of dependence on others. This was humiliating for a man who liked to keep his secret thoughts locked up inside him.

Certainly I was not frightened of him any more. No, I had really begun to love him though I had no way of showing it. His paralysed side, his large, white limp hand made me want to cry.

A few days later Effie said to me:

'I like to feel that Burr is a tiny bit better. I have been praying so hard about him. He tried to stroke my hand this morning but he has a lot of trouble in forming words and then, of course, I am a little deaf. So we are learning to talk to each other with our eyes, like youthful lovers!

'This morning the doctor sent a young masseur, who will try to bring back a semblance of life into his poor hand. He was a very nice young man and I wanted to be friendly with him. I said: "Look how the leaves of the trees in Kew Gardens are beginning to turn red. Soon we shall be in autumn. The sun looks very lovely on the water, don't you think?" '

'Yes, it probably does,' said the masseur. 'But I have no means of telling. I am blind.'

'I felt very humiliated but I had not noticed anything. He seemed to find his way so easily about the room. But afterwards I realized that Burr had known. Only Burr could not tell me. The one was blind and the other can't form his words. I realized that of the three of us, I was the only one to have no right to complain. It made me feel very selfish.'

It was then that Effie broke the inevitably sad news. They would have to leave the vicarage—the home they had considered as their own since the nineties. What a long, long span of life!

Burr's stipend would cease. He would no longer be actively a clergyman. This lovely vicarage would be pulled down, and Effie and Burr, just two more forgotten people, would go off in search of a house for their retirement.

Effie was opening drawers, sorting out old papers, slightly overwhelmed by the number of treasures that she was bringing to light. Many lay strewn, higgledy-piggledy, on her chaise-lounge. Here was a cryptic note from Prince Talleyrand-Périgord, that arch intriguer in French politics, to Nathan Rothschild, of Waterloo fame, dated 1831, saying in French:

Mon courrier n'est pas arrivé—mais je persiste dans l'opinion dans laquelle j'étais hier au soir—avez vous des nouvelles ce matin? Mille Compliments. Ce Jeudi.

My courier has not yet arrived—but I persist in the same opinion as I held last night—have you any news this morning? A thousand compliments. This Thursday.

I found it amusing to reflect that this echo of some long forgotten secret between two of the most picturesque figures in nineteenth-century European history should, thanks to Hannah and her female descendants, now flutter into my hands on my mother-in-law's chaise-longue in this modest vicarage.

There were letters from Sir Robert Peel to the Honble Henry FitzRoy, M.P. Berkeley Square, with great red seals at the back of the envelopes; from Lord Palmerston when Prime Minister to an older, sadder Henry FitzRoy who, broken in health, had offered to resign from his post as First Commissioner of Works. There was a photograph of Blanche Lindsay with her husband, Sir Coutts, on the lawn at Balcarres. They sat facing each other in the middle of this vast expanse with the castle behind a distant clumps of trees. He was wearing a stove-pipe hat, a dark jacket and light trousers; she a black cloak over a long, full white dress and a rather overpowering hat decorated with a rose. He was gripping a cane with both hands; she had a little white dog on her lap. Her features, incredibly young.

'May I look through all these and read the letters?' I asked Effie.

'Of course, child,' she said.

'I find a visiting card with the names of Hannah Mayer and her daughter,' I said, holding it up. It read:

Mrs FitzRoy
Miss FitzRoy
42 Upper Grosvenor Street.

Some of the letters were folded and sealed with wax; others had envelopes. I picked them up at random. State secrets and feminine chatter about children were deliciously mixed. In a folded sheet of notepaper was a lock of golden hair tied with a scarlet thread. Inside was written in Henry FitzRoy's manly hand:

A lock of Arthur's hair cut off to-day, he being sixteen months old. H.F. Paris, April 29. 1844.

A few years later this same Arthur writes to his Mama and Papa:

August 27.

My dear Mama and Papa,

I hope you are very well and happy. How is dear Grandmama to-day? I hope she will soon be well. I bought a globe yesterday which I think very pretty. To-day also, I saw the Eighth Hussars on horseback with their band. The music struck up a march. I am very well,

Your affectionate
Arthur.

'It would appear,' I said to Effie, 'that the great Mr N.M.'s widow had by then quite forgiven her daughter for marrying the man she loved, for here is her small grandson calling her "dear Grandmama".'

'She took Hannah Mayer to the church,' said Effie.

'As you attended our wedding,' I said.

'She certainly became quickly reconciled to the marriage just as I have become to yours,' said Effie. 'But that reminds me. There is somewhere a rather charming letter from Mrs N. M. to her daughter from Gunnersbury, in which she sends love and kisses to the children. Now what have I done with it? I saw it a moment ago.'

Effie searched amongst the untidily strewn correspondence and then exclaimed: 'Ah, here it is!'

24th August 1845
Gunnersbury

My dear Hannah Mayer,

We are now nearly established at Gunnersbury. I have been very much occupied for several days with the affairs of the establishment, not having any person to assist, but numbers who increase my occupation. I merely mention this as the cause for not writing, and really I imagine that my active faculties are not as they used to be.

Gunnersbury is, thank God, ready, the alterations are nearly completed, and wholly answer my expectations, and are satisfactory. The weather is fine and the gardens pleasant. Charlotte and her family are with me, and altogether the establishment settled. Therefore, we have reason to be contented and hope, please God, health may allow us to be so.

Lionel* is taking the baths in Germany. Nathaniel and his wife are staying at the same place for the same reason. They have the pleasure of each others' society.

Adolphe and Charlottee both returned here a day or two ago from Scotland and will shortly go back to Frankfurt. The wedding, I think, please God, will be celebrated in the middle of October. I have not yet decided whether I shall go. Charlottee wishes me to do so.

I hope, dear Hannah Mayer, that you are comfortable at Brighton. The weather is brighter and more agreeable than it has been. I shall be most happy to learn that our good Arthur is deriving continued benefit from the sea air. The weather now appears to be settled fine.

I recalled that I am still in your debt which I shall liquidate, I hope, one of these days. Can I send you anything now? Only let me know.

Remember me kindly to FitzRoy. My love and a kiss to Arthur and Blanche, and believe me sincerely, with affection

Hannah de Rothschild

* Lionel was her eldest son, *b.* 1808, *d.* 1879

When my mother-in-law had finished reading the letter, I asked her:

'Would the old lady whom the Moon saw being carried downstairs in a litter in the Judengasse at Frankfurt (the mother of the five sons who established banking-houses in five countries in Europe) have still been alive when Mrs N. M. wrote that letter, in which she appears to contemplate a trip to Frankfurt?'

'Gudula was her name,' said my mother-in-law, 'and she lived to the age of ninety-six. So yes, she would just have been alive.'

She took her pen and made a rapid calculation.

'She would have been ninety-two,' she said.

Now here was a very amusing letter from Henry FitzRoy to his daughter Blanche. It was a double sheet folded into six, sealed with red wax and posted from Baden on 7th August 1852. Inside was a beautiful etching of the Hotel Belle Vue at Wildbad, with ladies in bonnets and full skirts parading up and down in front of it, which was at the foot of high mountains. Henry FitzRoy wrote:

My darling little Pet,

I hope you are going on very well, and are very happy. I want very much to see you again, and hope to find you much fatter, and better than when I left you. Ma hopes to hear that you are the very best Girl in all Tunbridge Wells. Write me word if the two little teeth are coming down fast. We have been on a trip to Wildbad in Wurtemburg, a picture of which I send you at the top of this page. We drove all the time through the Black Forest, nothing but up hill and down hill all the way. We never saw anything of the black huntsman of whom Arthur has read and thought so much. We saw only children picking raspberries, strawberries and bilberries with which the whole ground is carpeted. It is very fine and may well be called the Black Forest, for most of the trees being fir trees, and the sides of the mountain being very steep, looking down into the valley is like trying to look into the night.

As we came home last night, it lightened very much, more brightly than I ever remember to have seen it, and the effect was beautiful. These dark glens and woods for a moment bright as with a Sun flash, and then again black as night. The view from the highest ground we passed over was very fine, we looked over the plain between the Forest and the Vosges mountains, with the Rhine running through it for many miles, formed a very pretty contrast with the darker and sterner scenery we were going through. Wildbad is a pretty valley with a clear, rapid mountain stream running through it. I hoped to catch some trout there, but it came on to rain, so that I could not. There are beautiful baths there where the water comes up fresh from the spring into the bath. The water is quite hot naturally. We only stayed there half a day and came back here. I do not know if we shall go anywhere else, or stay here till we come home. You must write and tell me if you hold yourself very nicely and are the best Girl in the world. Give my kindest love to dear Arthur. Tell him that I hope he is getting stronger every day, and that I send him one thousand good wishes. I will write to you again in a few days, and tell you what we are going to do,

God bless you, my darling children

Ever your affectionate

Pa

Two years later, Arthur, nearly twelve, wrote from Brighton to his sister Blanche, who had remained with her parents in London.

March 9 1854.   63 Marine Parade
                                                 Brighton

My dear Blanchy,

I thank you very much for your nice letter. I am glad to hear that you like Edgar Clifton; for my part, I am reading The Betrothed, and have just finished The Talisman. I like both very much.

How many dolls have you got, now that a new one has come from Paris? I hope you enjoyed yourself at the party; were there many little girls there? Mr Simms says that the primrose is to be watered every other day, but there is a fine camellia in Mr White's room. I have only been once on the chain pier.

It is not at all fine to-day, and if you have a yellow fog, we have a grey one. I write in my pocket book every day, but I keep a larger diary besides. It is very uncomfortable sleeping in my stays. I have a horrid gumboil which goes all up the side of my cheek. Tell Mama that as soon as we got her letter, Mr White got a filter for all the water we now drink.

Yesterday I began to drink beer at dinner, and I like it very much. We went to Folthorp's and (please tell it to Ma) they said that although it was their custom to consider the subscription continued so long as any book of theirs was in the house, yet they would make this an exception.

The boat I am making for you does not get on very well, but I hope still to succeed. I suppose that Mama has told you that I went in a boat on Saturday but that the 'Nelson' did not behave herself at all well. Do Mama and Papa intend to bring you to stay over Sunday at Brighton? If they do, write to tell me where, and if you can come at 2 o'clock, and we will order such a grand dinner for you, not such a one as poor Mama got but we did not really know she was coming. The canary and the bullfinch have asked me to enclose a note for Twee-wee, to whose mistress I send my best love,

And remain, Her affectionate brother,

Arthur FitzRoy

The note ran:

Dear Cousin,

I thank you very much for your letter. This is the first time I ever got a letter, and also that I have ever written one. I entertain as high an opinion of you, dear Twee-wee, as you seem to do of me. I believe you are of a bright yellow colour and sing very nicely. I wish they had taught me, but have you ever heard of brother Bully? Ah! He's the fellow for singing,

I remain, Your affectionate

Dick, alias Richard.

Shortly afterwards, Blanche writes to her brother:

Hotel Windsor
Rue de Rivoli
Paris.

My dear Arthur

I thought perhaps that you would like to have a letter from

140

me, so I write to tell you all about our journey, though I daresay you know everything by Mama's letters. We had not a very calm passage to Boulogne where we slept one night at the Hôtel des Bains, and came on to Paris the next day (Saturday) in a very comfortable coupé all by ourselves.

In this coupé there was a table, or rather a slab, and a looking-glass. I have been twice to see Uncle Nat [Nathaniel de Rothschild] who lives just beyond the Bois de Boulogne, but comes up to Paris every afternoon for two hours which Mama spends with him. I went to see a fair in the little town of Boulogne but saw nothing worth buying or that you would like. I hope you are comfortable at Everleigh, dear Arthur. I suppose it looks very nice now and that the rosery is in full bloom. Have you seen Princy, and does he turn round on his own axis in the same curious way as he used to, but I suppose you do not see him as you are not fond of little dogs. A *serjeant de ville* stopped us the other day to ask why Lily had no muzzle and to say she must have one.

We have a very sunny little apartment with a dining-room as well as a sitting-room on the *entresol*, and looking on the Tuileries. A great many soldiers go by here, and sometimes so early that they wake poor Mama at six o'clock. Uncle Nat has a very nice house and garden at Boulogne, and his house and Uncle James's are in the same grounds, which are very large and nice.

To-day we walked a little up and down the Boulevards but I could not see anything you would like. I hear that you have actually had the cruelty to kill, cook and eat a poor little bunny. I hope that you are well and happy.

    Goodbye, dear Arthur
      And with best love and a kiss,
        Believe me, ever your affectionate sister,
          Blanche FitzRoy

Then from the House of Commons, a letter from Henry FitzRoy to his son, dated 19th July 1858, one of the last he was ever to write to him. A few weeks later, Little Arthur died in Paris.

My darling Boy,

I am thankful to hear from Miss Wood that you are going on well. I was hoping to start to rejoin Ma this evening, but that is now impossible, and the best I can hope for is to leave at 6 in the morning, and that will compel me to remain at Cologne all Sunday, as I do not like to travel on that day. I hear that Blanchy does not at all approve of the German cuisine. The last chance she had (of tasting it) was roast veal with preserved bilberries which she thought came out of a Physic Bottle. In fact, one must make up one's mind to starve in Germany, as it is the only country in which there is not a single thing of any kind that is eatable.

I went to dinner at Lewes* yesterday, cold meat and salad in a tent. I dared not taste the salad as I cannot cure my diarrhoea. I hope yours is stopped.

As soon as ever I join Ma, I will write you word, how she is and what we are going to do. I think you will have to prepare for Paris for a few weeks, and I believe an autumn there would not be by any means disagreeable. Only, take care of yourself, and get strong enough for the journey, and then it would do you good. I have given orders for the book to be sent to you if they can find it.

> God bless you
> Your very affectionate
> Pa

My mother-in-law paused in what she was doing, and said:

'Yes, I recall being very moved by the letter you have just read me. Little Arthur was indeed taken to Paris. Do you remember how, in *Green Leaves*, Peli describes how Hannah was standing by the window of the bedroom overlooking the Avenue Gabriel (the maid having just brought Arthur's breakfast in on a tray), when he put down the big Greek dictionary he was consulting, and gently passed out of this world? So the autumn which Henry FitzRoy, then First Commissioner of Works in Lord Palmerston's

* Henry FitzRoy was M.P. for Lewes.

administration, had hoped would not prove to be by any means disagreeable, was to fill all their lives with sorrow. A year later Henry FitzRoy, blamed because something had gone wrong with the chiming of Big Ben, and broken-hearted because of his son's death, died at Brighton.

'So,' I said, 'poor Hannah was left alone with Blanche?'

'Yes,' said Effie, 'herself very ill and lying in that darkened room in the house in Upper Grosvenor Street in the drawing-room of which Blanche was soon to be married to Sir Coutts Lindsay.'

'What sad weddings they all had!' I exclaimed.

Effie looked thoughtful.

'There does seem to be a tendency for that in our family,' she said.

My mother-in-law returned to the sorting of sundry objects in her drawers. I continued to glance through the letters and papers already on the chaise-longue.

'Oh, look!' I cried. 'Here are some verses that Blanche FitzRoy wrote at the age of nineteen. They are a tribute to her mother and are written on the prettiest sheet of cream notepaper, with her name Blanche embossed on the top of the left-hand corner. They must have been written only a few weeks before her marriage.

> If I have nothing to give thee,
> 'Tis because I have given my all;
> My life, my love, my strength are thine,
> And my love is strong, tho' my strength be small.
>   Daily, hourly, mother,
> Would I shew thee my heart's fond glow—
> But the gifts that a mother cares to have,
>   Were they not thine long ago?
> March 10th 1863

Effie was still peering into boxes and drawers, adding to what she had put out on the chaise-longue. There were little bundles of letters written to Hannah by her Rothschild sisters and aunts in the early part of the previous century—all in very feminine writing with the old-fashioned 's' and very difficult at first to decipher, because as soon as one or other of them had finished filling up her four-page letter in this tall, delicate, spidery writing, she would turn the letter sideways and start all over again on top of the previous writing. Other bundles tied with tape contained an immense number of letters from Robert Browning and Tennyson to Peli, all starting: 'Dear Lady Lindsay'.

I asked Effie if she would be very lonely in retirement, but she answered that it depended what I meant by the word lonely, for had she not, in fact, been always lonely in the sense that unlike her mother, Peli, she had cut herself off from personal friends. Her immense faith that had hitherto sufficed her (apart from her love for her family) would doubtless continue to do so in whatever part of the country she found herself.

I told her about Mme Maurer (who appears in *The Little Madeleine*) and the fact that I had always had a particular affection for people older than myself. I had the impression that they had more to teach me. 'Peli, curiously enough, was like you', she said, 'so I fancy it is not unusual. Towards the end of her life she dictated many of her thoughts to my sister, Helen, of which I have here a copy. But by that time every succeeding year was robbing her of more friends, and she wrote:

"Pleasant it is in youth to enjoy friendship with those who are considerably older than ourselves; yet the penalty has to be paid. If we continue to live, they must needs pass on before us, and in after-years we become painfully conscious of many an empty place. Only memory remains."

Effie, who had been reading from the typescript in front of her those rough notes of her mother's, said: 'Here Peli tells of Sir John Millais's funeral. It illustrates her point:

'"Sad indeed was the sight of the procession which I saw on my way to the funeral at St Paul's ... the big palette and paint brushes swathed in crêpe. Sadder still the ceremony beneath the cathedral dome—more cheerless, less beautiful than had it been at Westminster Abbey. The service was half finished when Sir Edward Burne-Jones came in and took a place at no great distance from where I was. After he had stood there a few moments, during some solemn singing, I saw him grow deathly pale. He seemed to sway and I quietly left my seat and went to stand beside him. Tears were coursing slowly down his cheeks. 'It is terrible, terrible,' he murmured. 'I cannot bear it.' Then he added prophetically: 'Morris's turn next, and then mine.' A couple of years had not passed before those words came true."'

There remained G. F. Watts, who had painted that magnificent portrait of her.

'He rose at 4 o'clock each summer morning,' she said, 'not to be robbed of a moment's daylight. "I have nearly reached Titian's age," he said to Blanche, "I am in my eighty-seventh year!"'

'These moments with Watts left her with a tinge of sadness. He was almost the last of the great pre-Raphaelite school. Blanche's thoughts would go back to those afternoons that Sir Frederick Leighton used to give in his crowded studio, lit by one great window. What a host of celebrities gathered in that room! Tall camellia trees in full bloom and saffron-tinted azaleas half hid the pictures that would later be shown at the Royal Academy. Closing her eyes she could see again those pictures on their easels. Leighton's figures, when but half completed, were often modelled in subdued monochrome, and this seemed to send them into a far-away and ghostly twilight. Madame Neruda would ask Joachim to join her in playing a Bach concerto for two violins. Around the momentarily silent piano, in front of the fireplace, were grouped: Charles Hallé, who had probably played some of Chopin's waltzes; Piatti, one hand resting on the neck of his beloved cello; and tall, black-bearded De Soria, from whose liquid voice 'Bonjour Suzon' would shortly be demanded. A knot of painters stood hard by: Watts, Millais, Poynter, Burne-Jones, the Tademas, Val Prinsep and Holman Hunt. Robert Browning was certain to be near, closely following each bar of music and just perceptibly beating time.'

I could not get it into my head that before the end of the year Effie and Burr would have left the vicarage and that the house would be pulled down. It was as if at that precise moment I was already looking into the past as I had been when listening to Effie describing her mother's life with the Pre-Raphaelite painters.

She left me a moment to go to see Burr, and I wandered up into what had formerly been the children's school room.

What a bright room this was with its two large windows overlooking the river and the distant towing-path and the trees of Kew Gardens! But what I liked to do most was to browse amongst the children's books on those long yellow shelves. My own childhood in Clichy had been too hard for me to have an opportunity of dreaming the dreams of childhood. I had been too quickly introduced into the problems of womanhood. Inexorably drawn into the gossip of Matilda and her female friends I had been robbed of the fairy-tale atmosphere that I was only now beginning to yearn for. And here were all these absorbing, delightful fantasies that would almost certainly have been within my grasp had I been a richer little girl. I needed to have an orgy of fairy-tales as I passionately longed at this moment for Matilda to make me ethereal pink tulle dresses, or frothy creations of blue or cream chiffon, with bows and satin ribbons, so that I could fly away to the lilting tune of a waltz at Cinderella's ball.

8

MY NEW HOME HAD THIS LONG, narrow corridor onto which all the rooms opened, and everything was painted a glaring white as in an Atlantic liner. Painted walls, as a revulsion against wallpapers of the Edwardian home, or the Morris designs of Peli's day, were the fashion of the twenties, and so was everything shiny and hard like tables and doors of Lalique glass, which were quite the latest thing. As I had no experience as a housewife, and not enough money to indulge my fancy, I made do with what the decorators had left us. The largest room was at the far end of the corridor, and its huge windows formed virtually a semicircle, looking out both on Beauchamp Place and Brompton Road, and as the traffic was incessant both by day and night at this dangerous cross-roads, at which there were not yet any traffic lights, the noise and dust were at times unbearable, and drove me to despair. As we still had practically no furniture, and as it appeared to be the only room large enough to take the immense double bed that Effie had ordered us from dear Harrods, we turned it into the bedroom, and in order to dim the blinding light and lessen the noise, I hung heavy brocade curtains like a medieval tapestry against the bow windows at the back of the bed. We also saved up just enough money to buy a large natural wood wardrobe for my dresses and coats, of a simplicity then very modern, and a dressing-table to go with it. Even so one needed to be very young to accept both the noise and the cold of a new apartment in which there was no heating but the inadequate gas-fires which scorched one in front and left one shivering in the back.

Even though I had masked three of the windows with this brocade tapestry, there remained two, one on either side, and these in summer gave us lots of sunshine and the loveliest glimpses of the trees in Beauchamp Place and Brompton Road. The big new red London buses thundered along, put on their brakes at the crossroads, which were immediately below us, and then went off again when the policeman decided that it was time to beckon them on. The heavy vans and taxicabs did the same; while they were stationary their fumes rose like whiffs of poison gas. But when we came home late at night, or in the early hours of the morning, Pépé would be waiting for us at the roof-garden door, and leap up into my arms before I had time to take off my cloak or put down my handbag—and if it was cold we would all go to crouch in front of the gas-fire in the bedroom. If the motor traffic had died down, we might hear the clop . . . clop . . . clop of ponies bringing the small market carts from Brentford and Isleworth to Covent Garden with osier baskets full of garden peas, strawberries and fresh lettuces.

Meanwhile my mother in Stacey Street was beginning to lose her clientele, and even her friends. The Tall Louise (who appears in *A Girl at Twenty* and *Madeleine Grown Up*), following an angry tiff with her 'Mine', decided that she had put sufficient money aside to retire to Belgium. The Italian cook who worked at Claridge's and lived in the basement, unable any longer to endure the stuffy atmosphere, bought a small house in the suburbs for £500, which had a garden both front and back with a privet hedge and rose trees. He and his wife had always claimed that they would retire in their native country but having recently spent a short holiday there, they decided that they had become far too English in habit and taste to leave the land of their adoption. My mother felt that she was being abandoned by everybody and by me in particular. Though she had no positive views on what she wanted to do, she was incensed at the sight of all these people going off with their savings to enjoy a spell of well-earned leisure in pretty little homes of their own, while she remained practically penniless in her airless prison. My own peace of mind was shattered. Even though Robert had seen his salary suddenly increased to £18 a week (for the first time in his life) the expenses of moving into Brompton Road, with a crippling rent and no furniture, allowed me for the moment to give tragically little to Matilda, who imagined me living in a manner she had never dreamt possible for herself. On several occasions I had almost sobbed out my disquiet to Effie, but on reflection I was too proud. Had she not already overcome her own doubts on her son's marriage by giving me her affection? Besides, she was not particularly generous to her son. He had neither asked nor expected anything from her at the time of our wedding. In this respect he was adamant. Robert was not the sort of person to ask help of anybody. He would not easily have forgiven me for seeking charity— even for Matilda. He believed himself entirely capable, given time, of providing for all our needs.

The basement flat did not remain empty for long. Another cook who worked in the same hotel moved in and his English wife, left alone from early afternoon till late at night (that was the drawback of working in hotel kitchens) took a liking to Matilda. This young woman who had a gift, like so many Englishwomen, for making a place look gay, put up chintz curtains, and the kettle simmered on the hob for tea—not coffee. The couple were extremely happy, and their optimism being infectious occasionally helped Matilda to feel less bad. But the fact remained that many of her best customers deserted her, on purpose because of me! They claimed that as her daughter had married into money, there was no reason why Matilda should go on working. Those who had been nicest to us when we were just poor Madame Gal and her insignificant daughter turned almost venomous. One of the French girls who plied her trade in Conduit Street had seen me coming out of Asprey's in the grey squirrel coat that Robert had given me, and the news was quickly spread abroad and discussed by their maids over glasses of port wine at Bodega on Saturday mornings. How dared their dressmaker's daughter go about in a grey squirrel coat (then at the height of its beautiful fashion)— a coat that had come from Révillon, and had even been exposed as something special in the window. Of much of this I remained ignorant, but on meeting Virginia one day (a woman who sold hand-made lingerie and fine lynx skins to the French girls at their apartments in the morning while they were still in bed), she exclaimed: 'It is my duty to inform you, my little Madeleine, that your mother is having a tough time to make ends meet just now. The French girls refuse to give her any more work and gossip behind her back. She's as clever as she has ever been with her needle but what she needs to do is to set up business in a different part of the town. You ought to see to it.'

More than ever convinced that I must not broach the subject to my mother-in-law, who was not only anxiously nursing Burr but was also engaged in the very complicated business of looking for a new home of their own, I decided to bring Robert by stealth round to the burning question. I accordingly began to make it clear that there was something on my mind. At a carefully chosen moment I would give a deep sigh, and even allow a tear to course down my cheek. It may not have been a very honest way of achieving my ends but at least it proved a very effective one. I think he had never really understood how precarious her situation had become.

But even so there was no quick solution. At Stacey Street, my mother and I had paid ten shillings a week. Her rent had not gone up and I had, of course, no trouble in paying this, and indeed could have paid more, but such rents no longer existed, certainly not in Knightsbridge where I would find nothing under £5 a week, and that would represent an important part of our salary.

It would be dishonest of me to suggest that I was not having a wonderful time. We found ourselves invited to absolutely every-thing that was going on in town. Invitations came for At Homes in Mayfair, to garden parties, to art exhibitions, to theatrical first nights, to the opening of new restaurants, to banquests in the City. As we went out every evening, I had wonderful opportunities to wear the superb brocade dress that Matilda had made me out of the panels of Peli's ball dress, and it made me feel, curiously, as if I was in her skin. Though Matilda and I quarrelled, she never ceased to make all my dresses and even my coats. In fact it no longer mattered very much that her customers had left her. She worked increasingly for me and this made my moral obligation towards her all the greater.

When I had first gone to the Savoy, wide-eyed and naïve, I imagined that I was seeing all the secrets of a different, more glittering world. So I was, in a way. But now I was precipitated into something far beyond what my imagination could have allowed me to conjure up—into an international *mêlée* of Society, art, music and politics in which, in order to satisfy the needs of the Column, I was to meet all the great men and women of an epoch. Most of them, though now dead, remain, like those who peopled Peli's world, heroes and heroines in the book of time. I am surprised how adaptable I proved, but adaptability is a gift peculiar to young women. Everything in me began to change, to suffer a transformation, as if I had found myself once more at school and needed to learn my lessons all over again, to pass examinations. Robert's patience was infinite, and though presumably there were moments when he must have felt nervous about my reactions, he did not show it either by word or gesture. I had not, as the French girls believed, married into money but I found what I had always desired—a companion to guide me in a *milieu* where I could eventually make the best of whatever natural gifts I was born with.

We were invited one week-end to a very beautiful house in the country which Giordano, the Italian owner of Kettner's Restaurant in Soho, had turned into an elegant hotel.

I had known him, of course from my London girlhood, and my mother and I used to lean out of the window of our room in Stacey Street to watch him offering little bunches of violets to what we then thought the very smart women who drove up with their escorts to dine at his restaurant. He was very fat, a tremendous gourmet, and could make a salad-dressing quicker and more expertly than any man I have ever known, the greatest chefs included, but as he grew richer his absorbing passion, like so many Italians, was fast, expensive, shiny motor cars.

For this week-end in the country he sent to fetch us, his chauffeur at the wheel, an enormous Isotta, a machine that must have cost him an absolute fortune, but it was fast and extremely showy and that is what he wanted. As soon as we were clear of London and on country roads we shot forward, leaping over pot-holes, lurching from one side of the road to the other, making such a noise that people in the villages stared at us. The trouble was that Robert and I were seated in so-called luxury over the back axle, so that I was soon bruised all over. During supper, with all the garden lit up with Japanese lanterns, and the finest clarets and Burgundies to go with the various meat dishes, I began to feel terrible. Our bedroom was vast, newly decorated and I shivered in bed. In the morning I had a slight haemorrhage that did not worry me too much. My health was always so precarious, I suffered so continually from this or that, that I had become accustomed to suffering, supposing, as indeed proved to be the case, that I would never be entirely without it. As my periods were painful and difficult I took it for granted that I was probably having one a day or two early.

Back at Brompton Road, much against my will, though I was in great pain, I allowed Robert to call a doctor. It seems strange but we had none of our own. Robert had a thing about going immediately to specialists, and having telephoned to one of the great London teaching hospitals, he was given the name of their chief gynaecologist, who came round to see me.

The specialist was young and very good-looking but he took an instant dislike to me and roundly trounced me for a miscarriage that he was convinced was no accident. He said that I must go immediately into a nursing-home for a curetting. His obvious contempt for me made me feel perfectly miserable, and I caught sight of him looking at Robert with what I took to be pity, as if commiserating with him because he had married such an unprincipled young female, and this made me feel even worse, for on this score at least, I knew myself to be perfectly innocent.

As I had no choice, I went to his clinic behind the Natural History Museum in South Kensington, and looking back on it I can only think of it as being rather sordid, but this may be due to the fact that the nurses appeared to treat me with the same contempt as the surgeon. At all events I prevailed on Robert to come to fetch me as quickly as possible so that I could complete my convalescence at home.

Matilda never came to see me. We had had a stupid quarrel. Just before my week-end at Giordano's place, I had left Stacey Street, banging the door behind me. How bitterly I regretted this childlike behaviour, which deprived me of her love for several precious weeks. I had not yet learnt to swallow my pride, to apologize, even though it might not have been entirely my fault. Fool that I was. How could it not have been my fault! I who had both youth and happiness. I who was treating so abominably the one person I had loved above all others in this world. She had said something unkind to me and I had the temerity to reply that I had not asked to come into this world. She went very white, and I couldn't find the right words to put an end to the quarrel. I had wept all the way back to Knightsbridge—and then there had been the invitation to Giordano's new country hotel, and I had forgotten Matilda in the joy of choosing the right clothes for what I had hoped would be an amusing week-end.

Now alone in the big bed, with the curtains drawn behind me, Robert gone to the office, I had the terrible sensation of having been abandoned by everybody, considered as an object of contempt by the gynaecologist, by the nurses at the clinic. I wrote to Effie and told her what had happened. She wrote back by the next post:

Sep 9th 1931

My dearest Madeleine,

It was very sweet and kind of you to write me such a long letter, and to tell me so much about yourself; there is no reason at all why we should not write quite openly to each other, and I am grateful for your confidence.

If you had a miscarriage it should not leave pain afterwards, but it would certainly make you feel tired and ill, and you ought to rest as much as you possibly can for a time. Even at a very early stage such a thing is likely to be tiring and depressing, and requires a certain amount of care in the future. When you have pulled up your strength again, you ought to lead as healthy and normal a life as possible, but you ought not to get overtired, especially at monthly times, for fear of a repetition of the accident.

I am glad you are going to have a little holiday: —change of scene and plenty of fresh air will be good for you, and Bob needs a holiday also. Please stay away as long as you can—a very few days is not enough. Tell Bob I am hoping to send him £7 or £8 to help. A quiet place will be best for you, but it ought to be fairly comfortable and, above all, don't make the holiday too short for that, I feel sure, would be bad economy. Get him to make it a real holiday, and forget the *Evening News*, both of you; you will return all the fresher to your work. I will try to write later. Don't worry, my dear, about coming, I shall quite understand that you don't feel it wise to face even a little journey. I have torn up both your letter and your envelope, so no one will see them. Give Bob my dear love; I feel I am treating him rather badly but I felt I must answer *you* to-day.

God bless you, my dear, and strengthen and cheer you,
Much love,
Mother

I was now very accustomed to the part of London I already considered as my own, and when from my third-floor windows I looked down on Brompton Road with its old curiosity shops seen through the foliage of the trees, I was often intrigued by the name of Madame E, a court dressmaker, whose establishment occupied the first floor of a house opposite. One night when I lay awake wondering if I dared switch on the bedside lamp and read, which used to annoy Robert, who hated reading in bed, I heard from the direction of the Brompton Oratory a car seemingly travelling so fast that I was seized with indescribable panic. A moment later there were the most appalling cries I had ever heard—so terrible that I hear them still, the cries of a woman, almost inhuman, piercing the night, and the screech of brakes, and then the cries of another woman uttered in the split second before her impending death These crossroads deserted only a few moments earlier now presented a horrific scene, one body hurled over into Montpelier Street, the other dragged fifty yards farther on by the car unable to stop in time. The next morning Mr Lucy, the porter of our block of flats, told me that Madame E accompanied by a friend had gone out to exercise her dog before turning in for the night. It was while crossing the road on their way back that they had been mown down. After that we were given traffic lights, which made our crossroads safer but, with the resultant stop, go, of the traffic, tended to increase the amount of exhaust we inhaled without doing anything to deaden the noise.

At Brentford a cloud also hung over the peace of the lovely vicarage. Effie told me one afternoon when I had gone to see her that there was a house at Godalming in Surrey that might prove suitable but that as the owners had not yet moved out it would give her time to get everything ready.

What did they mean, these ominous words—that they would have to say goodbye to the garden with the raspberry canes and the mulberry tree so old that its mighty trunk had to be supported by a steel cable, but whose black fruit dropped so lusciously in autumn on the long grass? That Peli's pictures would be removed by alien hands from the walls of the dining-room and Effie's Little Room emptied of its chaise-longue, its glass screen, its family portraits and precious papers? That no children's voices would ever again be heard in the schoolroom where Mallalal had come to give her morning lessons and where I loved to look at those children's books on their yellow shelves?

I wondered if the memory of Peli, so venerated in this Thames-side house, could outlive the brutality of the move to a modern brick villa in Surrey. I had formed an almost passionate affection for this remarkable painter, poet and writer whose *Green Leaves* had first revealed her sensitivity to me, and whose paintings looked down on me in all the rooms of this doomed house, whose books I was beginning to know by heart.

I recalled a passage from the notes she had dictated to Helen:

'It was at Sir John Millais' house that I met Lord Houghton for the last time. He and Robert Browning were dining at Palace Gate; there was no other guest but myself. After dinner we sat in the studio. It was bitterly cold and Lady Millais retired to another room, but bade me stay on with the men if I liked. I sat wrapped up in a fur coat unwilling to withdraw. Millais smoked a short pipe, talking impetuously as usual; Browning's white hair and beard shone out into the firelight as he answered his host's remarks in a ponderous and reflective way; Lord Houghton, wearing a black velvet skull-cap, was plunged in a deep arm-chair, mostly listening. Millais, during the last few years of his life, would ask me to come and see his unfinished pictures and offer my criticism. "Consider it done," was generally his curt remark when I had suggested some alteration. Once he wanted to introduce a rose into part of his picture without delay. "Pink, just like the one in your hat," he said, laughing. "I could paint from that quite well." I therefore unpinned the rose. "As for paint," said Millais, to me in his joyous, debonair way, as he painted the rose, "I will say this for myself—there's no fellow living who knows better than I what paint can do. I won't talk about anything else, but I know how far paint will go and how to put it on canvas, and I don't care who knows that I say so." '

Then also these lines from *Green Leaves*:

'I remember a lovely picture, small as to size, painted by Sir Edward Burne-Jones, illustrative of the martyrdom of St Dorothea. In the foreground a brilliantly winged angel, bearing a basket of fruit and roses, is waiting on the doorstep of the house of Theophilus; in the distance, Dorothea kneels before the executioner.

'Roses are among the sweetest of flowers which are valued for their perfume even more than for their beauty. Many of us have treasured roses that have become wan and dry by age, whose scent still lingers and like some tender memory recalls bygone days, bygone affection, bygone youth and scenes and thoughts, in too subtle a manner for actual words.' And Blanche Lindsay quotes from one of her own poems:

> An old torn book, with one pale rose
>   Crushed in its yellow pages:
> I have not held it in my hand,
>   Nor read it thus for ages.
> Nay, formerly, the print was good;
>   Or else mine eyes were better,
> For now they're full of tears—too full
>   To see a single letter!

And as if foretelling her death:

> Methinks that you'll remember, when I die
> Not some brave action, nor yet stately speech—
> Though sheltered lives to these may sometimes reach—
> But just a turn of lip, a glance of eye,
> A trivial jest, a laughing word, a sigh,
> A trick too strong to cure, too slight to teach,
> Scarce noticed, haply mocked by all and each—
> Now a full source of tears you'd fain defy.

'But to those who have owned happy youth, beauty, riches, and all the good things of this world, it is indeed hard to grow old, to lose admiration, enjoyment strength and lust of life, to part with old friends and be passed over by new acquaintances, above all to bid farewell to what is called beyond all else love, warm human love and yearning, to stand by, physically and mentally colourless and unsought, whilst others, newcomers, and surely inferior souls, are praised and lauded—this surely is old age, and we are not well learned in the art of it.'

Effie, who was thinking about something quite different, said:

'I am giving the house we are to move into at Godalming to Burr. He hasn't enough money of his own to buy it, and it's a great joy to me to give him a present. He has never asked me for anything. He's just beginning to walk again, oh, so very slowly with the help of a stick and I fear that his hand will remain paralysed, but he has always shown an affection for Surrey so I think that the place may do him good. The garden is on flat ground though the house itself is on top of a little wooded hill above the railway station.'

I tried to discover what the house was called and to whom it belonged but for some reason she was evasive, and she was not the sort of person to allow herself to be questioned beyond what she was prepared to say. She had always, after God, been mistress of her own destiny, and I learned from her that femininity and strength of will are not incompatible.

Our apartment house in Brompton Road had five floors, each floor forming a single long apartment. We knew most of the tenants by sight by the mere fact of so often going up or down in the lift with them, but one day we were intrigued to find ourselves going up with a very smart liveried chauffeur, who told us that he was going to the third floor there to deliver a letter from his employer, a baronet, who was a renowned chess player, to his sister who was the third-floor tenant. 'Oh, but I know her!' I cried, mentioning her name. 'She is that charming woman who invited me to tea the other day.'

The incident would altogether have escaped my mind had it not been for the fact that the following Saturday we were to meet this same chauffeur at the end of a little path above Godalming leading to a small private estate.

'Hullo!' he said, 'I suppose you've come to interview Sir G . . .'

'Oh!' I exclaimed, not understanding.

'Why yes, before the great chess tournament. You write for the papers, don't you?'

'Because Sir G ... lives here?' I queried, trying to hide my surprise.

'Naturally,' he said, 'since you've found us here. But you're lucky to have come today because we've just sold the house—to a parson in Middlesex and his wife.'

I never told him that Robert was the parson's son and I his daughter-in-law.

But the garden was full of roses, and there was quite a lot of ground. Yes, Burr would surely be very happy here. But Effie would probably be furious if she knew that we had come poking our noses into her business.

9

THE HOUSE WAS CALLED WESTAWAY, and as soon as Effie and Burr were settled in we paid them a visit. My father-in-law, who wore a tie and a light flannel suit, could walk quite well on condition that he was not hurried and could take very small steps. I found him much less intimidating without his clerical collar, and I rather enjoyed our little walks round the estate.

He had discovered that by going to the top of the wood and looking down through the trees, which were mostly birch, he could at certain times of the day see a fast train from Portsmouth or Waterloo steaming past Godalming station. So there he would be, having cunningly brought me along with him, waiting for the sound of the still distant express, upon which he would take his gold half-hunter out of his waistcoat pocket, and say importantly: 'She's right on time today!' Followed by his pekinese, he would show me the rabbit warren, the apple orchard and the rose trees. The unfortunate little dog, innocent cause of his leaving Brentford, was probably as happy as he was at the change. Like its master it had become very old, and frothed at the mouth, which made it no less precious to Burr, who looked at it through the eyes of affection.

The estate, for that is precisely what it was, struck me as far too large for Effie and Burr—the wood, the warren, the immense garden, the lawns and herbaceous borders. The house itself was a solid brick mansion scarcely modernized but in which there was more than enough space for everybody. But as my thoughts were continually on Matilda, what put me in a paroxysm of jealousy was the discovery of a magnificent modern bungalow situated in the prettiest part of the garden and occupied by the young gardener and his wife—so much space, so much lovely country air, so many delights, for this alien couple to whom, because my father-in-law was so full of admiration for them, I took an instant dislike. Thus it often happened that our weekly visits to Godalming were in my case tinged with bitterness. I plundered the garden for fruit and vegetables to take back to Brompton Road, roses to put in the big Lalique vase in our bedroom. The young gardener looked on with the contented air of an employee determined to put to good use the infatuation of his naïve employers. With Robert and me he was distantly polite but at times suspicious, as if considering us as spies unloosed upon his secret domain. Already Effie had whispered into my ear that it would not be polite for us to explore that part of the garden in which his house was situated in case he or his wife might think we were trying to look through the chintz-curtained windows. Her words filled me with altogether unjustified resentment, for I wondered what qualities the gardener and his wife might possess which had allowed them so rapidly to captivate Burr's heart and her own. I admit that I only partly obeyed her injunction, for the path past their pretty little bungalow led to the wilder part of the garden with its old English apple trees and long grass full of primroses and cowslips in which the baby rabbits played, and there was also in my action a particle of revenge for the thought that these young people might have stolen away from me a corner of Effie's heart. I was beginning to regret the intimacy of Effie's Little Room at Brentford.

The great nuptial bed in which the children had been born had, at Godalming, been relegated to the guest room which, on our short visits, we normally occupied. It was a sad, cold room and even a coal fire in winter did nothing to give it a warm, cheerful appearance. The monumental bed with its brass balls and high legs looked absurdly out of place, for whereas in Victorian days people climbed up into bed, my generation and Robert's stepped down into much more simple beds whose mattresses were almost flush with the floor. On the wall opposite hung the very large outline for the portrait of Hannah which Ary Scheffer had started in Paris, when the beautiful nineteen-year-old girl, with her fair skin, blue eyes and small graceful figure, had gone over there in 1834 as the guest of her French cousins. It showed her as Prince

Edmond de Clary would have seen her when he fell so violently in love with her at the ball graced by the King and Queen of the French. Because I disliked this guest room at Westaway I thought it hard luck for this fine picture of Hannah (albeit unfinished) to have been relegated together with this absurd double bed to an unloved room. When it eventually came into my possession I had it taken out of its ugly frame, cut to proportion and re-framed in period pine so that it should hang always in an honoured place in my home. Many years later I was able to reconstruct with Lord Crawford during a visit to Balcarres in Fife how it had come back into the family. At the time of his marriage to Blanche, Balcarres belonged, as the reader will recall, to Sir Coutts Lindsay and it was to Balcarres that he brought his young bride who, delighted with all she saw, wrote back so lovingly and at such length: 'My darling Mama, You cannot tell how often I think of you now, how tenderly and lovingly.' Soldier turned artist, Sir Coutts had as a young man in Paris been a pupil of Ary Scheffer. At Balcarres, Blanche, turning over a number of canvasses in Coutt's studio, discovered this study in oil that was so evidently a portrait of her mother as a young girl. She ran to fetch her husband and asked him what it was. He told her it was an Ary Scheffer. After the death of the painter, he had decided to buy from Scheffer's Italian valet some example of his master's work. This was the picture that Blanche had found. Lord Crawford, who had taken me up to this studio at Balcarres, said: 'Both Coutts and his wife used to paint here. Coutts even knocked down a great slice of the wall to allow him to lower his larger canvases with the help of a pulley into the courtyard. Artists painted big canvases in those days.'

Effie and Burr now had twin beds. This allowed Burr to be more easily nursed and it permitted Effie, without waking her husband, to wander like a ghost through her house at night. She slept very little and employed the long nocturnal hours in tidying her chests of drawers, doing her accounts and reading— for she read voraciously and for hours at a time. She thus lived her busy life twice over—once by day and once by night. The day was devoted to her family, the business of efficiently running her household, of minutely watching over its daily expenditure.

But when night came the hours were hers, to read Pascal, the gospels in Greek and Latin. This was a trait in Peli's character that she had clearly inherited. Effie's sister Helen, recalling the hours she once spent with their mother after Peli had fallen down a stair at Hans Place, crushing a shoulder and giving her slight contusion of the brain, which necessitated her remaining for some time in bed, told me that Blanche had always preferred to read the Testament in Greek. One day as Helen embroidered a velvet binding for her mother's Book of Greek Gospels, she looked up and asked: 'What lettering shall I work upon it?' Blanche answered: 'He restoreth my soul!'

It was perhaps the fact that I slept badly in the country that I had taken this dislike to the guest room at Westaway. I actually missed the noise of the traffic under my windows in Brompton Road. Instead I would hear Burr's pekinese snoring in a closet where they put him for the night, and Effie's slippers as she shuffled from room to room, from one chest to the other. She banged cupboards and closets brutally, being too deaf to be aware of the noise she made. I would have liked to jump out of bed and to have followed her in her peregrinations—but life for everybody but herself had to stop at 10 p.m. at Westaway. At that hour punctually, whether we were staying there or not, Effie turned off the electricity at the master switch. Burr, who was terrified of fire, would never have slept if current were still running along wire behind walls and floorboards. Electricity was something mysterious that might at any moment short-circuit and set the entire house on fire. So after 10 p.m., if we really wanted to read, we had to light candles as at Brentford, and as Effie did, wandering from room to room with her lighted candle, sometimes softly singing hymns, a habit she had never cured herself of.

But, of course, we now had the radio, which had made big strides since Robert had worked on the *Daily Express* and had been unable to pick up signals sent out only thirty miles away from his listening post. All the family gathered round the large, cumbersome radio set to listen to King George the Fifth addressing his people at Christmas. Effie listened most earnestly with her head on one side and her Scots expression of taking serious things seriously—not joking about the King or the Prime Minister or Sir James Barrie, who probably reminded her of Balcarres when she had to break the ice to wash in of a morning. Peli used to tell about two wretchedly poor women in her Fife village. They lived in the same squalid cottage, one on the ground-floor, a hard-featured woman who went out daily to work in the fields, the other (the first-floor lodger) being bedridden and utterly helpless. They were in point of fact strangers to each other, but every morning before she went out, and every evening after her return, the ground-floor lodger tidied up the bedridden woman, 'redded her up' as the saying was, fed her and attended to her, never apparently growing weary of such kindly devotion. The question: 'Who is my neighbour?' did not trouble this ministering angel's thoughts—a ministering angel clad in coarse and ragged homespun, yet one of those who, in the future, may be accounted worthy indeed.

It seemed difficult for me with my flippant thoughts to equate King George the Fifth's halting and monotonous voice with the irrepressible gaiety of his four young sons, whom we continually saw dancing at Quaglino's or the Embassy Club—the Prince of Wales with whom all the women in the world were in love, the slim, handsome Prince George who danced so appealingly, the Duke of York and Prince Henry with whom Robert had been at Eton. No other country could boast of four Prince Charmings!

Mr Lucy, the porter at our block of flats, distributed the letters every morning. They came punctually at 8 a.m. with the milk that had arrived downstairs at 6 a.m. One morning there was a letter from Matilda in her neat little scrawl. My heart beat violently as I tore the envelope open. We were still having that absurd quarrel, and I was terrified that something might have happened to her.

In fact she did not say much—except that she felt lonely and that our quarrel weighed heavily upon her. When I realized the implications of these simple words, tears filled my eyes. I knew that I would never forgive myself, which indeed has been the case. It was not for her to mend the quarrel but for me. I should have run to her side long ago, knelt down and asked her forgiveness. What a terrible thing is pride! And then I had been taken off to that wretched clinic and spent all those days in bed at home, trying to get better. Why had I not taken a sheet of paper and written on it the one word: Come! I would do it now. She would get my letter by the afternoon post.

She arrived immediately—tragically altered, much thinner, her cheeks sallow and pale, but what I had forgotten was the colour of her eyes. Of an extraordinarily vivid blue!

This was the first time she had come to Brompton Road since I had altered the arrangement of the bedroom. She looked round and said: 'It's terribly noisy and you really should clean your windows, but there are so many that they would cost a fortune.' They were of the kind that you push up and down, and when the window cleaner came he sat on the sill and flicked his shammy-leather.

We both tried hard to pick things up where we had left off. Virtually all her customers had left her except for a girl who worked on the *Daily Express*. 'I think women must be buying their dresses ready-made,' she said, 'What do you think?' I really had no idea. Besides, I knew all too well why most of her customers had left her. So what could I say? 'How is your father-in-law?' she asked. 'Is he happy in his new house?'

'Yes,' I answered, not wishing to sound too enthusiastic. 'And the garden is very pretty.'

'I'm glad to hear it,' she said. 'It's a wonder what money will do!' I hung my head.

'But it's not easy to earn money,' said Matilda. 'What Robert makes doesn't appear to be enough for all of us. I ought to find a job—maybe, as a governess? There is this Englishwoman married to an Italian chef in the basement flat. She and I have become quite friendly. She has a sister who is housekeeper to a peer whose town house is in Mayfair. She invited me to tea the other day. We visited the house. It must be very agreeable to live amongst beautiful things, and even get paid for it!'

'You're not serious?' I said.

'The beautiful furniture, the plush curtains, the oil paintings—you have no idea. I would willingly spend my life in a house like that—a house with a family tradition! I'll show you one day. It's just behind the Green Park.'

I felt miserable. What could I say?

'She plays a very important role,' Matilda went on, determined to make me hear her out to the end. 'The peer has a wife and a mistress so that the housekeeper finds herself in the position of having to be arbitress between them. The wife asks her for news about her husband's mistress while the mistress slips her a five-pound note to persuade her to divulge information about the wife. Think of the money I could put aside with a good wage, no rent and a five-pound note now and again!'

'Oh, do stop it,' I said. 'We'll find a solution.'

'Of course, jobs like that are rare,' said Matilda, 'and there would be the servants to deal with. It's amazing the things I learn from this new friend of mine, and at least we talk English all the time. I am not sorry to be rid of the Tall Louise. I told you that she had gone back to Belgium? Unfortunately her room has been taken over by a couple who return home at all hours of the night so that they wake me up.'

Pépé had jumped up on her lap. She was stroking him and Pépé was purring. It was almost like old times, listening to her talking about the neighbours. I listened as I had always listened to her, entranced by her stories.

'Your darling cat, Nanny, has become old,' said Matilda, 'but she continues to have kittens.'

We heard the front door opening and Robert came in. He greeted Matilda rather sweetly but without surprise, and producing two tickets for the first night of a ballet, said: 'Here are two stalls for Covent Garden. Madeleine and I won't be able to go so if you felt like taking somebody?'

Rather to my surprise, Matilda said yes, she would like them—and put them in her purse, and as she got up to go, I whispered in her ear: 'Come back soon. Come tomorrow. I shall probably still be resting. My miscarriage has left me very weak.'

Robert took her to the door. He must have finally realized that Matilda's visit was in the way of a reconciliation. He said:

'It was nice of her to come. I'm delighted. Her visit will help to make you feel better. I bought a Scotch steak at Harrods for lunch on my way back from the office. I'll go and light the grill.'

We didn't often lunch at home so that when it happened it was almost a treat. The wine-shippers in St James's Street used to send us cases of claret and burgundy, and the champagne firms their rosé and non-vintage wines, so that we had quite a cellar. Though we never had any cash, we were terribly spoilt. For a girl in her early twenties it was like having stepped into the middle of a fairy-tale.

The next day Matilda came back as she had promised. She had taken her new friend to the ballet, Rossini's *Boutique Fantasque*, and both agreed that it had proved one of the most memorable occasions they would have to look back upon. Yes, they had lived through an enchanting fairy-tale; beauty, delicacy and colour had illuminated their existence when it had seemed to them most drab. And the music! There was an air in the ballet that she had suddenly recognized because everybody had sung and whistled it in Paris during those fabulous years before the war when Serge Diaghilev first brought his famous ballet there, surrounding himself with such artists as Bakst, Derain and Picasso, and musicians like Stravinsky, Auric and Milhaud. But what had made this air so important and poignant to her was the fact that my young brother (who was also called Robert) whom she had lost so tragically and at a more tender age even than Hannah had lost Little Arthur, had in his endearing childish way, hummed the air, or at least had tried to. And so it had made her cry—and she had cried practically all through the ballet, which was proof of how much she had enjoyed it—and not only had she and her neighbour made themselves very elegant for the occasion but they had been shown to the very best seats in the theatre—to seats in the middle of the third row of the orchestra stalls where absolutely everybody was in evening dress.

Robert, who had been witness of her enthusiasm, and delighted by it, told her of his experience ten years earlier when the *Daily Express* had given him that press pass for the entire season of great Russian ballet at the Alhambra, and he said:

'I can't give you in turn a pass for the entire season but I have just received two stalls for three more of the ballets, and I am sure Madeleine will be as anxious as I am for you to take advantage of them.'

Though as columnists it was not our function to be dramatic or musical critics we invariably received duplicate first night invitations to all the London shows, so that we could cover the social angle and describe the dresses of the women in the audience. But as we often had conflicting engagements that appeared more important to one or other of us for the next day's copy, we liked to give this small pleasure to Matilda.

So my mother went off very pleased with herself, and my heart was filled with happiness at the thought that our quarrel was at an end—though I was now determined to find her a suitable apartment close to our own.

I forget the name of the next ballet she was to see. I think it was *Casse-Noisette* but what I recall clearly was the anxiety with which I waited for her the following morning. She never came. I had spent a greater part of the morning putting my head out of the window to look at all the No. 14 buses, which stopped at the corner of Montpelier Street. I was certain she would arrive on a No. 14 because it was the one that came from the direction of Shaftesbury Avenue, and that was where she would board it. The ending of our absurd quarrel gave me such relief that I had now entered a phase as exhilarating as a honeymoon. The fact that I had waited all the morning in vain immediately filled me with new apprehension. Had I rejoiced too early? Would some former friend of ours have poured poisonous words into her ears? I could never be sure what they would do. I could, of course, have hurried round but Robert would soon be back from the office and we had our days and nights pretty tightly planned. We had an editor called FitzHugh of whom we were all rather frightened.

On my return home from some charity meeting of a committee of débutantes in one of those beautiful private houses in Belgrave Square, where Society women gathered over tea and cakes in the afternoon, I half expected to find a letter from Matilda. In this I was disappointed. But there was one from Effie. We had taken to writing quite often to each other. She wrote letters as naturally as she talked, and with no effort at all, merely allowing that fountain pen of hers to pursue its course over a pad on her lap. She talked about everything from the robins on the quince tree and the barges on the Thames to the favourite members of her mothers' meeting. Conversely she claimed that she had seldom read such amusing letters as mine, and she made me feel very proud by insisting that I had a natural gift for recounting trivial incidents in a light, particularly feminine manner.

So it happened that in a recent letter, having so often heard her talking about Balcarres, I had asked her in a postscript what had happened to it. I could not understand how an ancestral home in which so many members of her family had been partly brought up had so completely disappeared from general conversation. For, after all, I pointed out (by now having made myself reasonably familiar with her ancestors), General Lindsay who in 1823 had married Anne, the eldest daughter of Sir Coutts Trotter, had by all accounts not only lived there himself but brought up his children there—the future Sir Coutts, Robert, the future Lord Wantage V.C. ('Uncle Bob'), and their sisters, Margaret and Mary Anne. Subsequently Blanche Lindsay (Peli) had gone there as a young bride—and in due course Effie and her sister Helen had spent several years of their girlhood there, even complaining of having to break the ice to wash their faces in the morning.

To whom did it belong now? I asked Effie. In short why had it run away from my own Robert? Could it be that my query had been inspired by Matilda talking about her dream of becoming an indispensable angel in a peer's ancestral home!

'Yes,' said Effie, 'Balcarres had indeed run away from both herself and my Robert. I was quite right in supposing that General Lindsay cherished the place. Indeed he cherished it so much that he could not understand why his bride Anne Trotter complained upon being taken there for the first time of the evil smell of herrings hung up to dry on the house walls. She claimed they were a shock to her refined habits. In spite of what the General said about his home being a centre of cultivated and intellectually refined Society (which it was) yet the rather homely family life, the companionship of rigid-minded, puritanical maiden sisters-in-law, the society of rough-witted relatives and inmates who formed the entourage of Scottish households, were uncongenial to her. She was too fresh from the polished literary and artistic circle of her banker father's London home.

But of course she learned to love the place. Like all of us who are women we are adaptable by nature. It is a strength.

Besides, the general, her husband was right. Balcarres was a centre of intellectually refined Society—such men as General Simpson, who succeeded Lord Raglan as Commander-in-Chief in the Crimea; Sir Hope Grant; the Earl of Elgin and Sidney Herbert, who wrote: 'The refinement and high tone of everything at Balcarres strikes me more than ever.' Quite apart from this the deep glens, the long reaches of turf, the lofty crags, the rocky sea-coast, the dark caverns and the far-stretching sands, appealed to all the children.

Sir Coutts's and Uncle Bob's elder sister, Margaret, married her cousin, Alexander, who became the 25th Earl of Crawford. After Sir Coutts had left Peli, he re-sold Balcarres to the Crawfords, the elder branch of the family to whom, many years previously, it had belonged.

Thus did it happen, wrote Effie, that Balcarres had run away from Blanche and her descendants. Matilda would have to look elsewhere for a peer's ancestral home!

The next morning Matilda arrived.

She sat down beside my bed and recounted her appalling adventure.

She and her neighbour had again made themselves look very elegant to go to a ballet. They had become quite accustomed to these jaunts, and on each occasion they occupied the same excellent seats in the orchestra stalls. But not long before the final curtain my still so youthful mother had felt herself inundated with blood. She felt as though nothing would stop this dreadful haemorrhage, and her fear and anxiety about what would happen when she tried to leave the theatre were acute.

'Consider,' she said, breaking into tears, 'my friend and I after making a hurried departure, stood on the kerb trying to persuade the driver of a taxi to take us the few hundred yards that separated us from Stacey Street. He was the first of a long file of cabs waiting for the play to end, and he had been hoping for a worthwhile fare. He just laughed in our faces, telling us to walk. One did not hire a cab for so short a journey. Then we both tried to explain that I was unwell. I began to cry. He looked suspicious, and even turned nasty. 'Call an ambulance,' he said, 'I don't want to find myself with a corpse at the back of my cab!'

'In the end he must have had compassion on us—two unfortunate women, quite undone. He told us grudgingly to get in. I was far too afraid of inundating the back seat to sit down so I knelt on the floor, convinced that I was going to die before I could be helped out and up the stairs. Would I really present him with a corpse at the back of his cab? How would my friend get a message through to you? It was not yet midnight, and I felt certain that you and Robert would be out somewhere collecting copy for your next morning's column.

'But when my neighbour had put me to bed, I finally got to sleep, and this morning she came in early with a cup of strong tea with heaps of sugar. She said that it was the best remedy for what was the matter with me. In fact, I'm starting my menopause. My friend says that one can have the first signs as long as ten years before everything is finished—and I who wanted to be a governess to a peer!

'I must take you to a doctor!' I exclaimed.

'Oh, no!' she said. 'I'm not the kind who likes to consult doctors unless it's really necessary. We have to learn to live with our troubles. But for heaven's sake don't mention a word to Robert. Tell him that we enjoyed the ballet tremendously, and that if he has tickets for other first nights not to forget me. I need something to compensate me for what I've just gone through!'

She laughed.

I could hardly believe her swift transformation.

'Going in evening dress to a smart first night is so much more fun than going into a dark cinema,' she said. 'And my neighbour is so much gayer and more indulgent than all those foreign women in Soho. I am so glad you have become English. I'm not even jealous any longer of other people's happiness. Shall I go and make us a cup of coffee?'

She ran lightly down the corridor on her high heels. Heavens! how young she looked. She wore a black satin blouse with big white spots on it that might have looked sinister on any other woman, but on her, with her fine bust and tiny waist, it looked absolutely wonderful. And she had the slim legs and tiny ankles of a chorus girl. No wonder that so many people were convinced that we were sisters. Every time I see her after a short absence, I have the impression that I am discovering her for the first time. This fashion of short skirts suits her admirably and the sunshine lights up her golden hair.

When Robert came in I told him about Matilda's terrible adventure and he said:

'Well, that settles it. Let's find an estate agent.'

As I had been meaning to do just that, we ran across the road to a firm that advertised flats to let. I don't remember exactly how long our search lasted but in due course we found a very pretty apartment on the top of a maisonette in the same road as our own. Two large, airy rooms overlooked the leafy trees of Brompton Road; two others little private gardens at the back. So I signed a five-year lease in my name and put down the first instalment.

10

ATILDA WAS VERY SATISFIED with her new apartment. Her friend from Stacey Street often came to see her; together they explored the local cinemas, walked in Hyde Park, or took tea in the mansion in Cleveland Place with the peer's house keeper. Here they would be served by the footman with mustard-and-cress sandwiches, China tea and a slice of Fuller's famous walnut cake, of which there was always such a large supply, his lordship being very partial to it, that the two sisters would invariably pack one up for Matilda to take home with her.

My mother quickly made friends with the other occupants of the maisonette in which she lodged. Some, by a strange coincidence, she already knew. The brothers De Bry, celebrated for their chocolates, had divided their interests, one remaining in Bloomsbury the other opening a shop in Brompton Road. The Bloomsbury De Bry had married a French girl, the Brompton Road De Bry an English girl. The shop was not fifty yards from us, on the other side of Beauchamp Place, and it had a remarkable clientele, who went there for their coffee, their home-made chocolates and their delicious pastries. It remained open until quite late on Saturday nights, and if one went there at about 5 p.m. one could buy whatever cakes had not yet been sold at a very advantageous price, so that if I was in town I often went there. My mother, anxious to continue working, made several dresses for Mme de Bry, whose comfortable girth did not allow her easily to find what she needed in the shops, and as a result she was often invited to spend the evening with the De Bry family. M. de Bry, already past middle age, with his short stature and pointed beard looked exactly like the typical theatrical Frenchman, and was on excellent terms of friendship with his ambassador, M. de Fleuriau, who would often drop modestly in for a cup of coffee and a piece of M. de Bry's special chocolate cake. They would be joined by Prince Arthur of Connaught whom M. de Bry called 'Monseigneur' and who had a particular affection for this part of the town.

My mother started taking those long solitary walks which were to become such a feature of this period of her life. She loved London passionately and became familiar with all the streets and avenues between Knightsbridge and the Fulham Road. As she continued to like the cinema almost as much as in her youth when she had taken me to see the early Mary Pickford and Pearl White films, she would slip in to those small picture houses where she rediscovered something of the atmosphere of those romantic days.

The fact of having Matilda not only so near me but also of knowing her to be reasonably happy was a tremendous relief. She came to see me almost every morning and began making me some of the loveliest dresses I have ever possessed. At least she could be sure that I would produce her lovely handiwork at balls and receptions worthy of them, for I was increasingly precipitated into a veritable fireworks, which though nobody could guess so at the time, was to prove a terrible finale before another world war. Garden parties, first nights, operas, charity balls, receptions both in London and Paris, week-ends at Great Fosters with at least three of the sons of the King, an abundance of remarkable new books, new plays, new inventions made a scintillating contrast to the long, drab processions of workless, mostly from Wales, who marched wearily along Brompton Road with their banners on their way to demonstrations in Trafalgar Square. The London evening newspapers had become almost as literary as in Augustan days. Arnold Bennett, Dean Inge, Bernard Shaw and Lord Castlerosse replaced Addison and Swift. Were they the last years of the supremacy of the written word?

Matilda made our apartment a sort of second home. Not only was she constantly with me in the mornings but she took the place over when we went to the country, or to Paris or Berlin for week-ends. We had now put up bookshelves in one of the two smaller rooms, and she read avidly everything that came into her hands, not minding if it were in English or in French, mentally jumping from the books Marie-Laure had sent us to those that from modern English publishers constantly came in for review. At her place also she was often mistress of all she surveyed. Normally, under a clause in the lease, she shared a bathroom with a neighbouring tenant, and this was one of the reasons which had enabled us in the first place to discover such a charming apartment. The tenant had of necessity to be another woman. Perhaps they were not always easy to find. Matilda's neighbour was, she supposed, the owner of a West End club. She got up rather late in the morning, went out before lunch and did not return till last thing at night. A woman who lived in Bloomsbury came to tidy her flat every day, and look after her clothes. Matilda and she would pass the time of day together and invite each other to tea.

Meanwhile life had settled down for Effie and Burr at Godalming, and I no longer had any reason to be jealous of the big house, the lovely grounds or the gardener's cottage. But in many ways it was beginning to be a sad life for them, especially for Effie, whose mind was so accustomed to working at the Brentford relentless rhythm. As Burr could no longer easily be brought downstairs she made a sitting-room for him beside the bedroom and arranged a tall mirror to give him the added view of the trees in which nested his beloved rooks, cawing vociferously all day. He believed in an old saying taught to him in his boyhood that a house was lucky as long as the rooks did not forsake the rookery —and he probably thought that as long as he could see them and their nests life would continue as before.

One morning I had just finished reading the serial in the *Daily Mail*, as I did every morning in bed, when there was a ring at the door. What did Mr Lucy, the porter, want now? I put on a dressing-gown and went to see.

'Good-morning to you,' said Uncle George, 'your Auntie Nell has come to see you.'

Effie's sister, Helen, from her great height, beamed down at me with a very sweet, patient, affectionate smile.

'Oh, do come in!' I exclaimed. 'Let's go into the kitchen. I'll make some fresh coffee.'

Effie's sister Helen, three years her junior—born in 1868—with whom she had spent so many summers at Balcarres when they were little girls, playing in the garden or scrambling over the rocks, had in many ways been much nearer to their mother, Peli, than Effie had been. After Peli's death she went to China as a missionary and on her return to England married a Scot much younger than herself—Robert's Uncle George (and mine too for that matter) who dressed very much as if he were crossing the Highlands on a winter's day, and made me self-conscious because Londoners were apt to look at him in surprise.

But 'your Auntie Nell', as George called her also had her peculiar way of dressing. In her youth she was very beautiful. There is a magnificent portrait of her when she went to her first ball at Lansdowne House, when London was garlanded for Queen Victoria's Jubilee. It shows her with fair hair, a lovely expression on her almost Greek features, in a white, low-necked dress holding an illustrated medieval book of hours in her long, slender hands. At only fourteen she had shown unusual courage and initiative. Sir Coutts and Peli had parted, and there were money troubles. The Grosvenor Gallery had already cost Peli £120,000 of her fortune, and there were fears that the rest of her dowry might disappear with the artist she had so unwisely married. Had there been a son Peli might have been given better protection, but with two little girls, she felt terribly alone. Helen decided to save the situation. All alone, when most little girls of her age are at school, she went to New Court in the City of London to implore the help of her Rothschild cousins—and they were so surprised by the sight of this rosy-cheeked ambassadress arriving all by herself, in her pretty dress, that they succeeded, with the help of Uncle Bob, in doing what was necessary.

Peli moved with her two daughters to Hans Place, making two houses into one. The top of the house—Number 41—became a studio. In the summer of 1884, when Helen was fifteen, Peli painted a picture of the flower garden at Milverton Cottage, showing beds of brilliant Shirley poppies beside which stood a little black-gowned ghost of a person that was Helen

Sir James Linton, then President of the Royal Society of Painters in Water Colours, came to see Peli. Helen, who had been keeping her mother company, went upstairs to the room that she shared with Effie and with Miss Starie, a governess-companion. But neither was there. After a short time Blanche went up to the studio to fetch the picture of Helen and the Shirley poppies to show Sir James. On the way down, with the painting under her arm, she slipped on the stairs, from which the carpet had been removed because she planned to leave for the country on the following day. Helen and Sir James rushed to her rescue. She had fallen through a frail gate and the doctors eventually diagnosed a crushed shoulder and contusion of the brain.

During her long and terrible illness she was nursed by little Helen. With the stub of a pencil and by the light of a candle (not to hurt her mother's eyes) she took to dictation many of her best poems, and a book called *The King's Last Vigil*.

When finally she was well enough to convalesce in the country, she spent long hours resting in the garden, but her brain was as active as ever and, inspired by the lines of Herrick:

> Thy feasting-tables shall be hills
> With Daisies spread, and daffodils;
> Where thou shalt sit, and red-breast by,
> For meat, shall give thee melody.

She wrote a book about robins which she illustrated by a series of remarkable water-colours, many of which became classics. On the title-page she drew Helen feeding the birds. The book is also interesting because it reveals small sidelights on her character. Thus:

'A couple of years ago, on emerging from a dark room after a long illness, and much pain, I began slowly to recover amidst the sweet influence of a little country garden. The flowers that bloomed round me had been planted by a prodigal hand but according to no rule, so that, close together as they could grow, pressed the scented roses, carnations, lavender and sweet peas, flanked by a row of gaudy marigolds and hollyhocks on one side, and a low fence of gnarled old apple trees on the other. Beyond, though not very near, was a paling decked with cherries and currants, these latter always left hanging for the birds' benefit, and above its worn blue edge peeped the ancient red gables of the village inn.

'My little pleasance, though small, was sweet and fair to me; fair, above all, with the "various scene of thought" that John Norris of Bemerton, the 17th century writer, who wrote of gardens, knew and appreciated:

> Pleas'd with a various scene of thought I lie,
> Whil'st an obliging stream slides gently by
> Silent and deep as is the bliss I chuse;
> All round the little winged quire,
> Pathetic, tender thoughts inspire.

'The deep and silent Thames was indeed close at hand, though not actually in sight. As I sat for hours quietly, gaining strength but slowly, and in my feebleness not caring to move, the numerous birds grew to know me, and presently to lose all fear of me. Above all, I made friends with the robins.

'By and by, mine became a very garden of robins; if I walked they followed me, or hopped on in front, looking enquiringly back to entice me along the narrow path. When I fed them with crumbs, two pensioners would sometimes fight. Most especially I recognized amongst my daily visitors a very young and perky robin whose colouring was scarcely bright as yet, and another an old and strong robin. In combat the young one always had the worst of it, and was obliged to retire to a short but respectful distance whilst his senior greedily gobbled the bread. At last, however, the youngster resorted to stratagem. He arrived one day in company with a thrush whose imposing appearance frightened the old robin away. It was now the latter's turn to stand aloof whilst the young one with bold and defiant air, strutted under the lee of the thrush, and comfortably shared the meal.

'In later autumn the robins sang very sweet songs, answering one another, as is their wont, perching by preference on the tops of apple trees or shrubs, their heads erect and their beaks very wide open. Sometimes, at the end of a song, they would flop down on the gravel path at my feet, so that I almost mistook them for the falling red leaves of Virginia creeper.

'Meanwhile a kitten from the miller's adjoining garden made

friends with me. I had seen it tottering on the top of the boundary wall, mewing piteously till I approached and stretched out my arms into which it jumped like a soft silken ball, to settle itself on what became its favourite place—my shoulder.

'But the robins were offended. As I was sitting with the kitten on my lap, a robin alighted on a bough so close to me that I could have touched him, and then and there he sang a ditty of unmistakeable remonstrance. His bright eyes were fixed on his still innocent enemy.

'Many other birds came to my garden; nuthatches, blackbirds, thrushes, tomtits and so on; above all, doves who flew willingly down to be fed with crumbs. But the robins were my favourites, and as I sat watching them day by day, I grew more interested in their movements, manners and customs. Thus I could not but turn my attention to Robin-lore, and recalling in memory first one rhyme and then another, I began to search through my books, patiently, for further information.

'The robin seems an essentially English bird to us English people, perhaps even Elizabethan when we recall Dr Donne's description of

"The household bird with the red stomacher."

'Though he exists, of course, abroad.'

Blanche Lindsay had in mind a trip to Italy that she and Sir Coutts had taken shortly after the opening of the Grosvenor Gallery. Just then the poet Robert Browning was in Venice. Before leaving London, Blanche had sent him some songs that she had composed and he wrote to her thus:

My dear Lady Lindsay,

Shelley wishes in one of his poems for some world far from ours where music and moonlight and feeling are one: he must have forgotten that there was such a place as Venice, or rather as Venice might be. I found there moonlight and feeling in abundance—but music was altogether to seek—and now your goodness supplies the want most pleasantly. I shall associate your songs with the gliding on the Canale Grande and pacing up and down the Piazza, and forget the violin's purgatorial screech from the lower regions. Thank you exceedingly. As for your proposal to throw a little Venice colour on something of my own—all I can say is, you will probably enable me to hear, for the first time, that harmony and my verses do not altogether disagree, and I may even apply to the case some old lines that occur to me:

Lorsque de tes lèvres de rose
Mes vers échappent embellis—
Ô prodige, ô métamorphose!
Je les trouve presque jolis.

On this particular occasion, Blanche and Sir Coutts were accompanied on their journey through Italy by Arthur Sullivan, who kept on worrying how to write a Primer of Music that he had in mind but which seemed beyond him. 'How would you define a sound?' he would ask. But Blanche was already interested in the art galleries at Florence and—in robins! Yes, she also had a book on her mind. She wrote:

'It is impossible not to be struck amidst the loveliest woods and gardens by the extraordinary absence of singing birds. This silence in the heart of a beautiful landscape seems absolute desolation to a lover of birds. I remember the market place of a picturesque Italian town where the walls of the palaces, painted in fresco, were framed by shimmering blue hills. In the foreground, laughing girls drew water from an ancient marble fountain; figs, and peaches were profusely heaped in baskets all round them.

'My attention was called by a brilliant string of colour garlanding one booth to another. It consisted of dead bullfinches, wrens, thrushes, tomtits, greenfinches—and also of Robins!'

Blanche Lindsay recovered her health and the book came out. She gave the first copy off the presses to Helen—a Helen sweet and twenty and about to face that London summer season with its balls and drawing-rooms. Helen, in turn, gave this copy to me, saying that I would probably make better use of it than anybody else. On the fly-leaf under her mother's inscription to her, she wrote for me:

To my dear niece
Madeleine
with love from her affectionate Aunt Helen
March 1937.

So that once again, as so often at the vicarage at Brentford, I experienced a sense of feminine continuity in this family.

Now back to our story.

Well, here is Helen ('your Auntie Nell' as George says) in my kitchen, taking off a cardigan, then another cardigan, then another scarf, and so on and on.

'Peeling myself like an onion!' she exclaimed, laughing.

She struck me at first sight as massive, almost Wagnerian, and these tweeds and woollens she wore, of sombre, dull colours, hung about her untidily, and because her hands were partially paralysed, they fell white and inert from arms that appeared terribly long. In spite of this infirmity, owing to the fact that she had once been shipwrecked when a cross-Channel steamer went down at night between Newhaven and Dieppe, she managed to suspend from her person a quantity of brownish-red leather bags fringed like Red Indian work at the bottom and the sides, and into which she stuffed Bibles, tracts, books and scarves, like a hunter would put the hares and rabbits he had shot during the day. She was always of a delightful humour and her husband, who was twenty years her junior, was full of the most delicate attentions. She loved him dearly, gave way to his caprices, but ruled her little world by immense dignity and the softness of her voice. I had never felt shy in her presence as I had once felt shy with Effie. She loved all human beings irrespective of their class, their wealth, their poverty or their colour, and absolutely everything interested her. As indeed it did her husband. If one were to ask George a question and he did not know the answer, he would say in broad Scotch: 'I dinna know but I'll find oot.' She had delighted in her years in China, its vastness, its poverty, its immense beauty. She once said to me: 'Nothing in China is ugly!' She spread the gospel naturally, whether in China or in the King's Road, Chelsea, so that although her knowledge was vast it was not easy to have a flippant conversation with her. Everything had to be truth. She would never have told a young girl that she was pretty. Prettiness was knowledge and the state of the inner mind. When today I think back upon her, with her long skirts, her terrible coloured cardigans and Red Indian handbags I realize that she would no longer produce smiles in the street. She was dressed forty years before her time. Whereas I admit that there were moments when I felt awkward at the amused glances our visits produced at dear Harrods.

I installed her in the kitchen with a great bowl of freshly made coffee and a mountain of buttered toast, and I went into the room next door where the B.B.C. was due to start a German lesson which I followed. I knew Aunt Helen would like to be alone a moment. As she was a vegetarian, she was always hungry, and the buttered toast would keep her busy for several minutes. I put the radio on and got out my German book. I spent hours learning German and Russian in this way, and it was important not to miss a lesson. After a few moments I became aware that George had silently followed me in and had become as engrossed as I was. He too had a passion for learning, and so there we were both of us repeating the sentences after the German teacher in the studio. When it was over, he said: 'When one lives with a woman like your Auntie Nell, one spends one's entire existence at school!' We went back to join her in the kitchen and George repeated our lesson. She smiled indulgently, quietly prompting him, for she spoke German as easily as English and French. She had finished her buttered toast, declared it excellent, and was tidying the contents of one of her bags. She was learning Hebrew, perhaps in memory of her grandmother Hannah, but though she would certainly have allowed herself to be stoned and martyred in Berlin under the growing regime, her love for Scotland was as tremendous as her limitless admiration for Peli. Uncle George said:

'You know, Madeleine, every time I bring your Auntie Nell to London we have first to go and look at No. 41 Hans Place, and then I have to take her to Harrods and the London Library.'

Helen stood on the opposite side of the square looking at her mother's house in Hans Place as she would have looked at her grave. She saw again in her mind's eye all the painters, musicians and poets knocking at the door. Harrods was where she went shopping for Peli, and the London Library was the fountain of all wisdom. All the family were life members—Effie's Little Room was always piled high with those learned tomes, so clean, so beautifully looked after, with the red label on the front, which would arrive at the vicarage ten or twelve at a time in neat brown paper parcels.

Robert had arrived and now we were all together. When Aunt Helen spoke to Robert about Effie, she would say: 'your mother' in a very special tone of voice, and she would add: 'Your mother was always so dainty!' Her words surprised me, and yet they were true. Effie was smaller in stature, so neat that never a white hair was out of place, and her clothes were impeccable and smelt of lavender. 'I am not like Effie,' said Aunt Helen, 'I have never been able to discipline my person or my reading.' She had dived into her bag again and this time brought out between a Greek Testament and book in Hebrew a fat tome of legends and fairy-tales, of princesses, shepherds and metamorphoses.

'I will give it to you one day,' she said, 'but I cannot part with it just yet.'

When Aunt Helen first saw my son shortly after he was born, she exclaimed:

'He really doesn't look like you—or even very like Robert. He's exactly like the picture of Little Arthur. How Peli would have loved him, she who so longed for a son to make up for the brother she had lost.'

When he was four years old, she wrote to him:

'My dear little Bobby,
    Will you please thank your father for so kindly answering my letter and for sending the book to the sick lady to read. I think you have a little desk of your own. I have been looking through some of my things, and I found these Chinese paper figures, and I thought they would amuse you. The one in black and blue is dressed like a proper Chinese gentleman. In China he would be called a "read-book man!" He wears a long coat because he is not expected to do any field work, and his short black coat is part of a gentleman's dress and when I was in China was called a 'gwaché'—that is how it sounded. The little paper figure of a boy is wearing a violet coloured gwaché but the little boys often wear black ones the same as their daddies. The little

girl has the usual coat and trousers of a Chinese girl, fastened up the shoulder with loops and knots made of material, instead of buttons. See her plait of hair, tied up as usual with rose-coloured silk. The lady in green wears a skirt and a rather foreign looking dress so I think she is going out visiting. At home she might only wear a long coat and trousers, like the one in pink who seems also to have an apron on. I think she must be meant for a maid.

Your Uncle George and I hope that you are all very well. Are you going for walks in the park, and does your little dog still go with you? When I was a little girl, I used to like the Flower Walk best but that is in Kensington Gardens, a long way from you. We had a French *bonne* called Elise and she loved to *faire le tour de l'eau* —which meant walking round the Serpentine. But I was only a small girl, and I used to get very tired walking so far. The flower walk was lovely, with its patches of bright flowers, and lots of seats to rest on, and other little children to watch. We didn't go to the Green Park where you go.

I told you that I was looking through my things. I found some verses written by Peli—your great grandmama—and I think I will copy them in case you would like to learn them:

> But a little child am I
> Yet I call to Christ on high.
> Without fear, for it was He
> Who said: Let children come to me.
>
> He that understandeth all
> Knows how weak I am and small;
> He who was himself a boy
> Knows child-sorrow and child-joy.
>
> Daily will I make my prayer;
> Me and mine keep in Thy care,
> Guard us, Lord, both night and day,
> Guard us with Thy love alway.

Do you learn hymns? Which do you know? I like:

> Gentle Jesus, meek and mild,
> Look upon a little child.

and

There is a green hill far away.

Goodbye, Bobby dear,
Much love and kisses to you and your Mamma and Father,
from Uncle George and Tante Hélène.
XXX

II

I REALLY NEVER KNEW if Burr was pleased to have a grandson. When, after fleeing from the German Army in France, I arrived, holding the baby in my arms, in the room where he was resting at the house in Godalming on a hot June day, it was difficult to read what passed in his mind. Effie had greeted us affectionately. The baby was terribly heavy, and struggled in an effort to get down and try to walk, which he had not yet learnt to do. His cheeks were pink and bright and his little arms and legs still golden from the hot sun of a French summer.

For Robert, the child and myself, this lamentable flight was humiliating in the extreme. We literally no longer had a penny in the bank and the ground-floor apartment he had brought us back to in Shepherd Market, Piccadilly, though compact and modern, was even more sparsely furnished than had been the one in Brompton Road when ten years earlier we had first moved into it. On the outbreak of war in September 1939 Robert had given up both our own flat and my mother's and sold the furniture, thinking that with the baby we would be safer, if London were bombarded, in Normandy. He had spent the intervening months in a lodging-house in Clarges Street, not expecting that France would be defeated and that he would have to bring us back—the baby and myself—as refugees, leaving my poor mother stranded on the quay at St Malo.

On this hot June day, therefore, I stood before Effie and Burr with the child in my arms, feeling as if I had done something wrong, and was being judged. Which indeed was the case. My miserable position was witness that all Burr's misgivings at the time of our marriage were justified. Though on my return, as the prodigal daughter-in-law, nobody had slammed the door in my face, the Surrey air was heavy with irony. France had lost the war, its armies were in full flight and its politicians were making a dishonourable peace with the enemy. Robert and I had been married for ten years, and had nothing to show for our labours. Though we were not back to ask for charity, which nobody would have given us anyway, we would soon, if Robert lost his job because of the war, face a future as precarious as it was possible to imagine.

I needed to be very young to bear so much indignity on frail shoulders. The sight of a beaten army is something never to be forgotten, soldiers throwing away their rifles, tearing off their insignia and getting drunk on golden beaches. The land of Napoleon brought to its knees in scarcely less time than it took Hitler to conquer Poland. And now for me to have to admit that I left my mother alone, and in tears, on a hostile and dangerous shore. Had I been older shame would have killed me.

Without a house of my own, without money, without my mother, without a single plan for the future, I stood there listening to the rooks cawing in the tree-tops in Burr's little wood. That old feeling of jealousy rose up inside me. The garden was full of roses in full bloom, the country air smelt good and the big house was at peace—except for the occasional gurgles of the baby, while on the other side of the Channel my house was being pillaged, perhaps burned, my personal belongings divided up among thieves, my coats and dresses carried off by strangers.

'I think I'll go out in the sunshine a moment,' I said to Effie. 'It would be nice for the baby.'

We went as far as the gardener's cottage with the chintz curtains and the lupins. What would I not have given for such a fairy palace! In my imagination I saw myself cooking lunch, sewing, gardening, making Matilda comfortable in a rocking-chair—just as in those children's stories on the yellow shelves of the school-room at Brentford. My mother had bravely crossed the German lines and found a deserted rowing-boat on the sandy beach. She had come safely back and was now holding out her arms to take the child. What a beautiful dream! What a poignant awakening!

We had tea in the dining-room, which was icy cold on this summer day—and quite appallingly sad. The baby began to cry, then to scream. Effie looked surprised, and then pained, as if she had forgotten what babies do. Or perhaps she had never known, for in her youth there were nannies, governesses, nursery-maids. There was no longer a pekinese in the house. It had grown so old that it had been put to sleep.

But soon there began for me a new and wonderful life. At night during the air-raids we crouched (the baby held tightly in my arms) under a table in the hall while all our windows were blown out and the half dozen chairs smashed by blast into small fragments, the bare walls pitted by jagged glass, but in the daytime when the raids had ceased there was all that delightful gossiping with other women in the Green Park while the baby was learning to walk. I had never realized what fun one can have without a penny in the bank, and not much hope of living till the morrow.

Effie wrote me the most delightful letters, she would even telephone me in the early mornings after there had been some particularly heavy raid. She never invited me to go and stay with her but if, perhaps, I subconsciously felt slightly aggrieved at this, I learned later to be immensely thankful. She had guessed in her infinite wisdom that my family—myself, the baby and Robert—must stand together and forge our own protection against the world. And that even when Robert was away, as he often was, I must learn to stand on my own. So much that I know now I owe to her. London, with a baby, in the middle of a battle, a battle for its very existence, was a much more vivifying place than a gardener's cottage in a dormant Surrey garden. She wanted to give me the qualities of the women of her race, women who knew how to stand up for themselves and be proud. What a cold winter this winter of the bombing. I have this short word from her: 'Yesterday Connie went to town and brought back one poor little pound of rice for a month but we have plenty to eat. Your cake and chocolate are a wonderful addition—just luxury—to which the food controller says we have no right at all, and indeed my conscience agrees with him. So don't keep sending them. Lots of love to you, my dear Madeleine, and to the little lad.'

Christmas was over and soon we would be celebrating the New Year. The date was Sunday 29th December 1940 and Robert, home from the office, put on his tin hat to go fire-watching on the roof of our block of flats. From time to time he would come back to tell me what was happening. As I had a baby I was allowed to do much as I pleased, though in fact I took the baby about with me everywhere like the Chinese women who strap them to their backs. I had no intention of leading a sheltered life. This proved to be a memorable night. Over a hundred enemy planes showered incendiaries on the area between St Paul's Cathedral and the Guildhall. The flames would go on burning until practically nothing was left of what is known as the City of Milton and its medieval churches, so many rebuilt by Wren.

This is a night that historians will recount every time the glories of London are written: the Plague of London, and the First and Second Great Fires of London. Thanks to Effie I lived in London that night.

In the early hours, Robert walked down White Horse Street and when he came back he said: 'The whole town smells of damp plaster and burning wood, and I have just seen a man propped up against a wall in White Horse Street. I wasn't sure whether he was drunk or dead. I was too afraid to find out. What cowards we are.'

It was about 6 a.m. and I was already starting to make coffee. I said:

'Don't worry, all the drunks of the Green Park have taken to sleeping in White Horse Street.'

Though the City was burning furiously, the West End was enjoying glorious peace after the racket of the night, and everybody was exhausted. Only the baby had slept soundly and was now jumping up and down in his cot, making a terrible din. The telephone rang. 'You'd better answer it,' I said to Robert. 'I'll try to keep the baby quiet.'

He took off the receiver and began listening. I saw the blood drain from his cheeks and he sat down limply on the side of the bed. He had made a curious little noise, as if emitting air from his lungs. He turned towards me and said:

'Effie says that her Burr died in the night. In the small hours peacefully.'

I heard him say into the phone: 'I'll come just as soon as I can.'

He came back the same night but said very little. Burr who was so terrified of thunder and lightning had died at the end of the greatest explosions his beloved City (he had worked there as a curate before going to Brentford) had ever known. No thunder had ever rolled more loudly, no flashes of lightning had ever been so terrifying. Robert said: 'Effie keeps on doing what she has to do as if nothing had happened but from time to time she goes to look at him, as if he were merely asleep. She has never been more dignified than in her grief. She is worthy of all those dour Scots of her noble race.'

But Burr was English and I bought dozens of English red roses to put on his grave: that he should go to his rest with the red rose of England on his breast, the red rose of his land, and which is now my land.

I saw very little of Westaway after Burr's death. In London the war was closing in on us, and we lived from hand to mouth, our window-panes smashed and replaced by a sticky, tar-like material; two or three rickety chairs; the baby's cot—though Bobby was no longer a baby and beginning to walk—and the double bed which Effie had given me when I first went as a bride to Brompton Road, the only piece of furniture remaining from that apartment.

Early in the New Year we hired a car and went to Godalming. Effie must have heard us coming up the drive because she was waiting at the front porch, and we flew into one another's arms. She said: 'You must not cry for Burr.' By which she meant that he was in Heaven. She had aged, found it difficult to climb stairs, and the house was too big. The cook, whom she had brought from Brentford, had left to marry a train driver, and the parlour-maid was a girl soldier in khaki.

Nothing in Burr's final dispositions allowed us to suppose that he had ended by judging Robert and me less severely than the day he refused to marry us, or even to attend our wedding. And yet, after his death, the safe he always locked so carefully (making a great show at night of shaking the handle to be sure it was properly closed) was found to contain nothing but a very worn Teddy Bear that Robert had loved when he was a child! Effie told me that she had decided to put Westaway, which she had given him, up for sale. Presumably as a sign of continued reproof we were none of us—Robert, the child or myself—mentioned in the will.

Later, Effie, rather shyly, gave Robert Burr's gold half-hunter with which he had timed the trains from the little wood—but the gift was from her. To me she gave a cardboard box in which she had put his dressing-gowns, more especially the one in Jaeger wool she had bought the day we had gone shopping together in Knightsbridge. The gift of a man's dressing-gown seemed incongruous at the time but I expect that she was trying to tell me that I was clever enough with my needle to re-cut the beautiful material into something feminine. After the war, when Matilda and I were reunited, my mother made a coat for me out of the Jaeger one which I had dyed navy blue. The material was so superb that I still wear it on occasion and then I think with affection of Burr. I doubt if I ever quite succeeded in making him love me.

The new house was called Leusdon, small but quite attractive, and which formed part of a housing estate near Charterhouse. We went there to wish Effie happy returns on her eightieth birthday. How proud she was to have reached this age.

The small drawing-room in which she spent a good deal of time had those same paintings on the wall that had made so great an impression on me when I first saw them in the dining-room at Brentford. I also recognized many things from her Little Room overlooking the Thames. Her basket and her Bible remained always at her elbow but she no longer knitted. The war was still on and dangers seemed to surround us. Our future seemed bleak. Helen and George, who lived near Norwich, seldom came to town. Aunt Helen had fallen while hurrying to answer the telephone during an air raid. When George, who had been fire-watching, returned home he discovered her on the floor with a hurt ankle.

In Effie's garden the lavender was in full bloom, and I felt a great urge to take her in my arms and kiss her lovely forehead. There was a book open on her lap and when I peeped over her shoulder (she still wore those Shetland shawls which I shall always associate with her) I recognized it as *Green Leaves*. She had turned to the final issue of these quarterly pamphlets—the one numbered 35, which Blanche Lindsay had been preparing during that summer of 1912 before her sudden death while Effie and the family were spending their holidays at Folkestone. The subject was about growing old, and Blanche Lindsay had been reflecting on those words by Owen Felltham, the seventeenth-century essayist, to the effect that it was bad enough to grow old but a great deal worse to be both old and ignorant. In short, that a foolish old age is a barren vine in autumn whereas a grey head with a wise mind is a treasure of great precepts. But it was not this that Effie appeared momentarily concerned with. I had caught her reading a poem of Peli's quoted in this final pamphlet from an earlier book of hers. It was called 'An Old Woman's Faith' and it was about the sorrow that a widow must constantly endure when thinking back on her beloved partner. What had moved Blanche Lindsay to write this poem? Had she been thinking of Hannah, the Rothschild girl's sorrow on losing her beloved Henry FitzRoy? Or was it prophetic insight into this present sorrow that Effie was enduring, now that she spent long, solitary hours thinking back on her dear Burr?

Nay, but the time's too short to fret—only a few more years—
What's the use of grief or regret? Where's the comfort of tears?
He went yesterday to the grave—I shall follow to-morrow;
They that travel so fast and sure may not bandy words with
    sorrow.
Well, you say that I don't heed much—yes, you have said it, and
    dare
To count me heartless or hardened of heart, while you that
    scarce knew him, can care!
You with your youth and beauty and friends, and a thousand
    gifts of earth,
I who'd but one thing left to love, and had learned to know
    its worth.
Yes, for our forty wedded years that passed like a breath on the
    sea,
Were better than empty words or sobs—better for him and for me;
And if hope cries loud from the human breast that we'll live
    and meet again
In the mystic land where there's never a tear, never a twinge of
    pain,

But where we're to clasp each other close and look in each
    other's eyes—
Smiling to see youth's smile renewed, forgetting old age and
    its sighs—
Why, I'd better sit still and think—think of the joy to come,
And patiently fold my hands and wait.

When spring came round again, Effie wrote:

'What lovely weather! One evening I went to the farther side
of our field, and picked a few primroses that were growing under
the trees. Each year at Brentford, as Spring came, I longed for the
sight, and smell, and touch of growing wild flowers. God has
given them to me now, and I often think that I am not grateful
enough for His mercies. There was a little rough corner under a
wall in the Vicarage garden at Brentford where Dad planted some
primrose roots to please me. We called the corner "Cornwall",
and tried to think it looked like a country lane.

'I only remember once being in Scotland—at Balcarres—
during the Spring of the year. I think I must have been about
11 or 12, and the joy of it has never faded from my mind. There
were masses of primroses, and there were bluebells, and red and
white May trees, and laburnums. It looked like Paradise but I
suppose I saw it through a child's eyes. Flowers and trees have
been landmarks in my life.'

12

EFFIE DIED VERY PEACEFULLY on a couch in her drawing-room at Leusdon.

Just before her death, while the war was still on, she wrote me the following letter, which brings to a close this affectionate and poignant study of daughter-in-law mother-in-law relationship.

Leusdon
Godalming

Dearest Madeleine,

I must try to write you a letter that will be as much as possible like a talk; I wish we could have a real chat! Perhaps some day you will be able to come to see me, but just at present travelling with the child would be difficult, and we can never be sure of getting a taxi from and to the station.

I was not expecting Bob on Saturday; I happened to be looking out of a window when he came to the front door, and I was pleased to see him. I had nothing nice to give him for lunch—only some half cold mutton, and a couple of tomatoes.

I think Bob must have been tired when he got home; he seemed quite happy when he was here, but I suppose he had been working in the morning for he told me that he had come straight from the office.

There is so much I would like to say to you, but it is difficult to know how to say it. I think you may be quite sure of one thing, and that is that Bob really loves you very dearly; he is like his father in many ways, and Dad was a very faithful friend—if he once loved, he never altered. Quite a little while before he left us, I said to him: 'Do you love me as much as when you married me?' He answered: 'Yes, but much more!' But though I always knew—and felt *quite* sure that he loved me—he hardly ever talked about feelings, and—in many ways—was very reserved. Bob talks a great deal more than Dad ever did, but I don't think he talks much about himself, does he? and you probably have to take a good deal for granted, as I had to do. Then you have an added difficulty to deal with, and that is that Bob has an uncertain temper, and is often very irritable.

It is wrong to be irritable—it is bad for oneself and for those with whom we live. It is a fault that is hard to overcome, and the best way of meeting it in others is *not* to mind too much, and to pray that the bad tempered one may be helped by God to overcome his weakness and to grow in grace.

One small bit of comfort I can offer you, and that is that Bob certainly is more even tempered and happier since you and he married, also I am sure that the child gives him a sense of responsibility that is good for him; and he is so fond and proud of the youngster.

I think the war atmosphere makes everyone feel rather down, and—at times—as you say yourself découragée. The amount of wrong and hatred in the world must have a bad effect on everybody. Minds and bodies are tired, and there is nothing very bright to look forward to. We must—as Lord Salisbury used to say—study large-scale maps.

Some time, in the future, God will bring good out of all this evil; He does not plan it, or make it, but He over-rules it and bends the man-made evil to serve his purpose. So we pray day by day: 'Thy kingdom come,' in the sure and certain faith that it will come, and that we shall see it and rejoice in it, either 'in the body or out of the body', to use one of St Paul's expressions.

'I can quite understand, dear Madeleine, that, at times, you feel home-sick for the country that, after all, is yours. But 'home' is not really so much a place as an entourage. It is where those we love are at any given time.

I have had quite a lot of dwelling places: —first in Scotland and in a London house—in Cromwell Place, then after a few minor moves—Hans Place; later on the Mildmay Deaconess House— then Brentford; after that Westaway—and now here.

This house is less of a home than any because he who made the home is no longer with me. Now I know that the real home—

the 'abiding city' is where the Lord Jesus is 'preparing a place' for his people. Meanwhile I am sure that He wants us to be happy in whatever earthly home He has placed us.

Don't type too much, dear Madeleine—you might hurt your hands and that would be bad for you. If you find they are getting tired or cramped, give them a rest for a few days. I have read about the socks made on two needles, but I never made any. I think you do wonders in the making of small garments for little Bobbie; he always looks most comfortably clad. I am glad he liked the book.

If you ever find you can spare a few hours let me know, and we will try to arrange matters. I am writing this in bed at night and it is nearly 2 a.m. so I must settle down to sleep. I wanted this to be such a nice letter—just all for your dear self; it is not as nice as I meant it to be but it takes you a great deal of love.

May God bless you and give you strength and courage, and love and patience—new grace, day by day, to meet the ever new needs,

Mother

The End